Imagining
the **Twentieth Century**

Imagining the
Twentieth Century

Edited by Charles C. Stewart and Peter Fritzsche

Contributors

• Walter L. Arnstein • James R. Barrett • Donald E. Crummey

• Kenneth M. Cuno • Kevin M. Doak • Peter Fritzsche

• Poshek Fu • Nils P. Jacobsen • Blair B. Kling • Diane P. Koenker

• Mark H. Leff • John A. Lynn • John P. McKay • Kathryn J. Oberdeck

• Leslie J. Reagan • Paul W. Schroeder • Charles C. Stewart

University of Illinois Press

Urbana and Chicago

Publication of this book was supported by a generous grant from Jerry Nerad, LAS '64, University of Illinois at Urbana-Champaign.

This book is printed on acid-free paper.

Library of Congress
Cataloging-in-Publication Data

Imagining the Twentieth Century /
edited by Charles C. Stewart and
Peter Fritzsche.
    p.   cm.
Includes bibliographical references (p.   ).
ISBN 0-252-02317-X (alk. paper). —
ISBN 0-252-06663-4 (pbk. : alk. paper)
    1. History, Modern—20th century.
2. History, Modern—20th century—
Pictorial works. I. Stewart, Charles C.
II. Fritzsche, Peter, 1959– .
D421.I38 1997
909.82—dc21   96-51311
                              CIP

Sally Mayman/Tony Stone

Contents

Preface

"At five miles an hour, I felt I was flying"

"everything is so much better now"

"the war changed my whole life"

"back then there was still a sense of anticipation"

"of course the most important thing was getting married and
    having children"

"it's always the same: the rich get richer and the poor get poorer"

"I will never be able to trust them again"

"we had so much hope"

"when I was growing up, dear, we didn't have technology"

There is no resolution to the compelling conversations about the twentieth century. Injections such as "still," "of course," "never," and "always" indicate very different ideas about change and time. The exclamations, opinions, and memories of people who have lived in this century confront and contradict each other. It is as if they were amateur snapshots assembled and pasted into a vast photo album of modern life.

The photo album or the scrapbook is perhaps the best way to introduce the twentieth century. Recent history is inescapably autobiographical because the reach of political catastrophe, technological innovation, and economic pressure is so great. As one series of these photos indicates, even the smallest children were enrolled in the discipline of civil defense. One common note to the twentieth century is the fact that two world wars, political revolutions, and mass-media "imagineering" have had near global impact. Never before have so many people been uprooted, drawn to new opportunities overseas, thrown into exile, and thus forced to construct autobiographies out of discontinuities—

"Born in Romania, she immigrated to Israel in 1974"
"my father Pedro Mendez Villarreal was born in Spain in 1905"
"my uncle came to Zanzibar from Oman to export cloves"
"we only knew after he died that he had made up most of his life
    in Glasgow"
"Camela Gioiosa was born on May 18, 1917, in Ripacandida, at the
    top of the hill"

—Not surprisingly, the images we call up in our minds when we try to make sense of this tumultuous century are bound to draw on personal life stories more than on any dispassionate account of places and events. Private lives and public histories have intermingled to create all sorts of very distinct and often very vernacular versions of the last one hundred years. This certainly was the experience of seventeen professional historians at the University of Illinois at Urbana-Champaign who spent the 1995–96 academic year together studying the meaning of the twentieth century. Under a grant funded by the National Endowment for the Humanities, this seminar explored "the fate of the twentieth century" and then put together a team-taught course for college students to convey the findings of those meetings, to be taught each semester until the end of the century. Another offshoot of that seminar is this book, an album of snapshots that seeks to distill the essence of our collective study of the century.

The result is a frankly unauthoritative history, which has the virtue of being true to the many voices of the twentieth century, to the losers as well as winners of political contests, to Africans and Asians as well as Americans and Europeans, to ordinary people as well as famous leaders, to those who express satisfaction and surprise as well as outrage and despair, to people who still give hope and to others who must account losses. As the seminar participants considered the images that they felt best portrayed the significant events, the ideas, and the personalities of the century, it became clear that a march through the front pages was inadequate. While watershed political events that are familiar to most readers—World War I, the rise of Nazism, the atomic bomb, the disintegration of the Soviet Union—are featured, our historians found slower-moving changes in private life, in sexuality, in family structures, and in our increasing ability to manipulate nature and technology equally important. This drift away from political history is a sign of the profession's own movement, but it is also a reflection of the inherent autobiographical slant to our work. That is why this "history book" resembles a private photo album which chronicles father's military service but also the family's first automobile, which celebrates sister's graduation but also memorializes new toys and the latest fashions.

This collection displays other biases as well. Our contributors are evenly divided among specialists in the non-Western world, Europe, and the United States. But in our efforts to imagine the century we found ourselves giving a bit more voice to the northern hemisphere simply because it was from this arena that so many of the century's dramatic changes emanated. We have probably given less attention than it deserves to the globalization of the world economy that so distinguishes this century, but it is the nature of autobiography that bank accounts and cash flows do not really alter the significance of people we knew and the meaning of places we have been. In short, this collection makes no pretense of being a representative history of the twentieth century. Yet its tentative nature rings true. In conversations with friends and relatives and in the oral history projects of our students we have been struck by the fact that the eyewitnesses to the century do not think of it as a progression of world leaders and dramatic declarations. What has remained in memory is a sense of vertigo in the face of the mobilization of social groups, the extension of technology, the flexing of state power, and the libertinism of the individual. Rather than stepping into the march of human progress or leading to the climax of political drama, *Imagining the Twentieth Century* follows the odd passages, side doors, and cavernous attics of our collective memories.

We are indebted to the National Endowment for the Humanities for the sponsorship of the seminar out of which the idea for this volume emerged, although this book received no funding from that source. It is to our fifteen colleagues who helped locate images and who wrote essays for this collection

National Archives 47-G-3C-2105

that we owe an enormous debt of gratitude; we have all dedicated our royalties to the Department of History's Graduate Student Fellowship Endowment. One of the great friends of the department, Jerry Nerad (LAS '64), has also dedicated his support for this project, and we gratefully acknowledge his confidence. We appreciate as well the help provided by the dean of the College of Liberal Arts and Sciences at the University of Illinois, Jesse Delia. Our research assistant, Christopher Hannauer, helped the project along at crucial points by tracking down photographs and permissions. Thanks also to Peter Michalove. It was the vision of Richard Wentworth at the University of Illinois Press and the design work of Ed King that finally ushered this photo album into existence. Finally, we are beholden to Karen Hewitt and Séverine Arlabosse, who were each particularly influential in their confidence and their encouragement that a book like this would be fun.

Charles C. Stewart

Peter Fritzsche

Imagining
the **Twentieth Century**

Private Histories

"My dearest," confessed Johanna to her husband, Julius, in early September 1914, "we're now writing to each other more than we ever did when we were courting." What prompted the flurry of letters was the outbreak of World War I, which mobilized the middle-aged shopkeeper from Hamburg, separated him from his young wife and small daughter, and shipped him off to the eastern front. Until Julius was killed in action six months later, husband and wife wrote one another almost daily letters, sometimes penning long and heartbreaking confessions, other times scrawling a few short lines on a postcard.

Johanna and Julius were hardly exceptional. Every single day in the wartime years of 1914 through 1918, wives, sons, daughters, sisters, brothers, mothers and fathers, teachers and friends sent some ten million pieces of mail to the front lines, and every day soldiers sent about seven million letters back, an extraordinarily intense production of personal accounts of living in time of war. The Germans alone sent a total of twenty-nine billion pieces of mail between the battlefront and home front. At the same time, parents took souvenir snapshots of mobilized sons, and wives pasted together private scrapbooks of their husbands' battlefield progress. If the periods of happiness are the blank pages of history, as Hegel surmised in his *Lectures on the Philosophy of History,* then seasons of unhappiness generated page after page of handwritten history.

War forcibly enrolled private lives in great public dramas and encouraged participants to make links between the personal and the political. The more protracted the conflict, the more turbulent its various scenes; and the clearer the ideological stakes, the more people felt the violence of history and fashioned their own tentative versions of events. Although thousands of books have chronicled the wars of the twentieth century, the private archive depicting soldiers' departures and family homecomings is far vaster. It includes the countless photographs and letters and mementos of better times that have been recollected in periods of loss and places of exile.

Overseas migration, imperial expeditions, World War I, the Russian Revolution, mass unemployment, the rise of Hitler, the division of Europe, civil war in China, decolonization in Africa—no century has acted with the violence of the twentieth century, no century has torn people from their remembered pasts with such finality, no century has so unsettled economic and social lifeways, no century has insisted so ruthlessly on ideological conformity. In this rough turbulence, the private histories—the letters, the scrapbooks, the photo albums—that families assemble depict the collisions of private and public lives, the treasured encounters and subsequent losses.

Technology has of course aided the effort of writing the self. Literacy and

Ullstein Bilderdienst

post roads in the eighteenth century contributed to the rise of the letter; photography, and particularly the snapshot, made it possible for even ordinary people to create a portrait gallery of the past in the nineteenth. Yet technologies only permitted what the soul sought: memory in the face of loss, personal recollection in the face of public eventfulness. The photo album is emblematic of the fate of the twentieth century. It tells the story of violent rupture in private lives and of the insistent recapitulation of ceaseless change in private terms. This very book is an attempt to sift through the countless vernacular versions that twentieth-century history has produced.

Peter Fritzsche

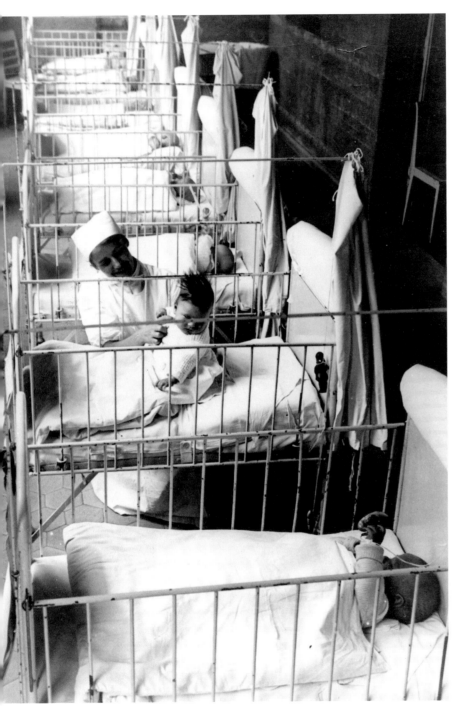

Birth of a New Age

The twentieth century was marked by an unprecedented population explosion. A whole new category of young people has broadened the base of demographic pyramids across the globe. Algiers, Mexico City, and Manila teem with children. This explosion in the number of births has aroused fears of mass starvation in the Third World and prompted dire predictions of ecological disaster on a global scale. To date these dystopian visions have not come true. What is certain is that the tremendous pressure of numbers throughout most of the Third World was caused in part, and inadvertently so, by nothing less than a medical revolution in world history.

Western Europe and North America pioneered modern preventive medicine in the nineteenth century, but it was only after the World War II that this medical revolution was passed on to Africa, Asia, and Latin America. Third World governments found that modern methods of immunology and public health were often simple and inexpensive, but extremely effective. One famous measure was spraying DDT in Southeast Asia in order to control mosquitoes bearing malaria, one of the globe's deadliest and most debilitating tropical diseases. In Sri Lanka, DDT spraying halved the yearly toll of deaths in the very first postwar decade at a modest cost of $2 per person. Deaths from smallpox, cholera, and plague declined by more than 95 percent worldwide between 1951 and 1966.

Asian and African countries also increased the small numbers of hospitals, doctors, and nurses that they had inherited from the colonial past. Sophisticated medical facilities became proud symbols of national commitment to a better life. Yet these facilities usually benefited a small urban elite. Critics maintained that expensive medical technology was an indulgence that Third World countries could not afford, for it was ill suited to the pressing health problems of most of the population. Such criticism eventually prompted greater emphasis on delivering basic medical services to urban slums and the countryside. Local people trained as paramedics now offer reliable prenatal and postnatal care in many rural districts.

The expanding medical revolution in the Third World continued to lower death rates and lengthen the average life expectancy. Of great importance, children became increasingly likely to survive their early years. As in Europe during the nineteenth century, a rapid decline in the death rate was not immediately accompanied by a similar decline in the birthrate. Until the 1980s, Third World women in good health generally continued to bear from five to seven children each, as had their mothers and grandmothers. Between 1950, at the onset of the global medical revolution, and 1975, the combined populations of Asia, Africa, and Latin America increased from 1,750 million to 3,000 million (and surged to above 5,000 million at the end of the century). In the same quarter-century, population grew much less rapidly in the old industrialized nations. As a result, the overwhelming majority of earth's people now live in the Third World. The twentieth-century person has become undeniably younger, more apt to be African or Asian, and more secure in health and well-being.

John P. McKay

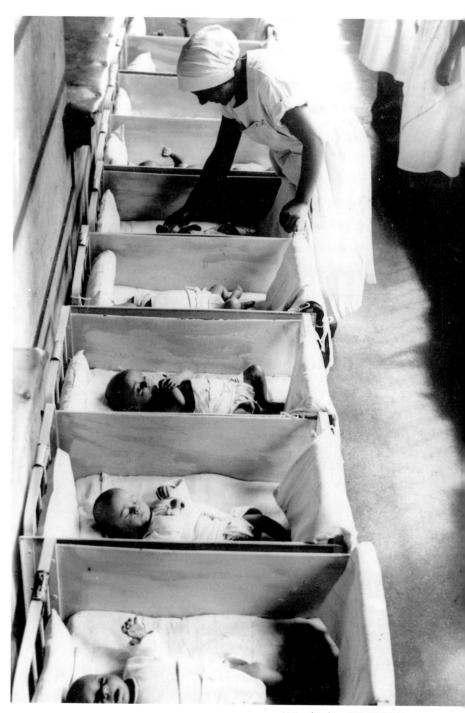

Childhood

For the world has lost his youth,
and the times begin to wax old.
—Second Book of Esdras, 14:10

They probably did not know that scholars and statesman had christened theirs "the century of the child," but their faces, peering out at us from the squalor of Chicago's stockyards district just after the turn of the century, convey the promise of a new age. Just as Freud and other theorists placed increasing significance on childhood to explain not only individual but also social development and pathology, professional reformers and governments took increasing interest in children's health and prospects. One effect was an expansion of "child-saving" legislation and agencies—labor and family law, juvenile courts and reformatories, structured recreation and sports programs. Another was the growth of compulsory public education along with John Dewey's and Maria Montessori's child-centered curriculums and other pedagogical innovations. At the end of the century primary education is universal, secondary education extremely common.

The grandchildren of these stockyards kids also grabbed the world's imagination. The post–World War II "baby boom" brought with it the child-centered family advocated by Dr. Spock and other pediatricians. As the "boomers" matured, they transformed their generation's popular culture, sexual mores, and politics. Yet this postwar demographic bulge and the centrality of youth culture were aberrations to some degree. Birthrates have fallen in the West for most of the century, though these figures have been somewhat countered by economic growth and the welfare state which brought much lower infant mortality and longer life expectancy. The world remains filled with children; up to 45 percent of populations in many Third World countries are under age sixteen.

Growing up has never been easy, least of all for "other peoples' children"—the poor and minorities. Because they were poor, these Chicago children lost much of their youth to child labor. Their siblings often died in infancy. Today child labor, sexual exploitation, high infant mortality, and new contagious diseases—all remain serious problems in developing nations. Even in the United States and some parts of Europe, the poverty rate among children is on the rise, while increases in divorce and drug and alcohol abuse are depriving even more privileged young people of community and family supports that often sustained these stockyards kids through crises. War has returned to Africa, the Middle East, and Europe, and with it technology and terrorist strategies which mean that such conflicts affect children more at the end of the twentieth century than they did at its beginning—emotionally and psychologically as well as physically. Today's city streets in America and Europe can be nearly as dangerous.

Is it possible for today's children to sustain the innocence and hope of these stockyards urchins in the world we have created? Will the century of the child end with the disappearance of childhood? We read the promise of a new age best in the faces of our own and other peoples' children, children with and without shoes.

James R. Barrett

Servants

Servants set the tables, scrubbed the dishes, and made the beds when the twentieth century turned, but they disappeared out the backdoor within just a few years. Easily identifiable in 1900, hard to spot in 2000, kitchen maids, butlers, and gardeners remind us that much of the social revolution of modernity that historians associate with the last two hundred and fifty years really came in this century. One hundred years ago, roughly four out of five people in Europe and North America still belonged to the working classes and many of these worked as servants. In the United Kingdom, in 1911 the world's most urbanized nation, one out of every seven employed persons was a domestic servant. One out of three British girls between the ages of fifteen and twenty worked as a maid or a cook for someone else. At the beginning of the twentieth century, it would not have been off the mark to choose a servant as the average person.

An ordinary trade, domestic service was a difficult livelihood. Servants were poorly paid, for there was always plenty of competition for available jobs. As a result, schools for servants, like this one in London, sprang up to teach young women the manners and household skills that employers in the "servant-keeping classes" demanded. These English girls are going to class, learning to wear starched uniforms, to polish door knockers, to mop the front stoop.

Moreover, domestic servants worked long hours and had limited personal freedom. For the full-time general maid in a lower-middle-class family, there was an unending routine of babysitting, shopping, cooking, and cleaning. In great households with many servants, the new maid was at the bottom of a rigid hierarchy. Abuse and unwanted sexual advances were occupational hazards. Not surprisingly, turnover was rapid; in Berlin around 1900 half of all ordinary maids found a new employer or a new line of work within a year. Young servants dismissed without references turned not infrequently to temporary prostitution or petty crime.

Yet domestic service had real attractions, especially for country girls with strong hands and few specialized skills. Wages were low, but they were higher than in hard agricultural work. Marriage prospects were also better, or at least more varied, in the city. Many a young domestic made the successful transition to working-class wife and mother.

These ancient routines and rigid hierarchies fell apart during the Great War of 1914–18. In the 1920s, it was a rare family that enjoyed the services of a full-time maid and it was a rare young woman who agreed to the long hours and dull tasks of household work. The vast mobilization of soldiers and workers and women during the war favored the spread of egalitarian ideologies and broke down social conventions. What the twentieth century fashioned were great national publics in which citizens recognized neither servants nor the aristocrats they often served.

John P. McKay

Ethnicity

Ethnic peoples were invented as much as they were discovered by the twentieth century. Processes as diverse as anthropological investigation and nation-building, colonial administration and neighborhood associations, increasingly sought ways to classify people with shared experiences. When these experiences were most easily described as cultural traits but fell into subsets below the notion of race, the group was often identified as a distinct ethnicity. More and more, ethnic identity overrode other collective identities such as religion or economic function. Ethnic groups—the Germans, the Americans, the Japanese—soon made their way in the twentieth century as completely natural and eternal entities. This presumption of ethnic coherence has had extraordinary political implications.

The ambiguities inherent in the newly discovered idea of ethnicity are

Courtesy, The Field Museum, Neg.#13223, Chicago

well illustrated by this first photo of an Ainu family which had been brought to the 1904 Saint Louis Exposition as part of the Japanese exhibit. The Ainu were an indigenous people who lived throughout the Japanese archipelago but were driven to the far northern part of Japan by the late nineteenth century. What made the Ainu worthy of exhibit was the fact that the darker-skinned Japanese majority found these light-complected, hairy, and European-featured people quite as strange as Bantu Africans regarded their pigmy neighbors, or Europeans, generally, had long regarded Africans. The way in which Japanese have seen the Ainu, well represented by the bearded old man in the photo, reverses the customary racial hierarchy observed in the West in startling ways: anthropologists even maintained that these backward indigenous people were racially Caucasian!

Making distinctions between peoples is, of course, as old as human history. But in the twentieth century, new, supposedly scientific techniques coincided with forceful political claims. Ethnicity became such an important way to think about the makeup of the world because the vast transformations of the modern era have spurred a fascination with indigenous, primitive, and "backward" groups. But even more important was the political project of building powerful states on the basis of the shared culture of ethnic nationality. This trend raised key questions about people's identity in a state and about the rights of the state to acculturate people into ethnic nations or to exclude inhabitants as non-nationals or as ethnically alien.

The construction of ethnic identity had a tremendous impact on twentieth-century history. Both world wars involved competing claims of nationality and ethnicity. World War I resulted in part from ethnic peoples who demanded ethnically determined states (Serbia for the Serbians); World War II pitted those who insisted on creating a new world order of ethnically homogeneous nation-states (Germany, Italy, Japan) against those who did not (the Soviet Union, Great Britain, the United States). After 1945, decolonization movements made strident ethnic national demands as a way to achieve political independence.

The Ainu in Japan remind us that the problem of ethnicity was more complicated than simply the rise of clearly defined but subjugated nonwhites against white imperialists. Ethnicity dispersed identities within races; nations were not simply out there to be enfranchised. As nations were made, ethnic identities were alternately manufactured and denied in an ongoing, often violent struggle. Just how artificial ethnic identities sometimes are is highlighted by the debate over the "Stone Age" Tasaday people in the Philippine rain forests. Are they as authentically primitive as some anthropologists have claimed, or did they fashion a public identity calculated to catch the eye of outside visitors and to fit the ethnic-based categories of census-takers and Western anthropologists? However these debates are ultimately resolved, the representations of the Tasaday and the Ainu remind us of the originality, the plasticity, and the volatility of ethnic identities in the twentieth century.

Kevin M. Doak

Anachronism

Wyoming Division of Cultural Resources

Indians and apartment dwellers, pow-wows and petticoats. When in human history—other than in the twentieth century—have we ever seen such a juxtaposition of human cultures and lifestyles? Wild West shows, like the Buffalo Bill Wild West Show of 1906 (pictured here) began in the mid-nineteenth century, but achieved their greatest popularity between 1880 and 1914, after the Indian wars were over and while the belief in progress was still persuasive. The closing of the American frontier had captured the imagination of the world, and these Wild West shows proved particularly popular among Europeans who, like the spectators in the stands, were comfortably distant from the "savages" and could look on the spectacle with bemused nostalgia mixed with pride in their own modern modes of social organization.

But pride always combined with melancholy. One can imagine the happy escape to the open frontier that such shows provided industrial workers who dreamed of freedom in a more primitive (but more human) kind of life than what their dark and dirty factory jobs afforded. What did the tenement dwellers, whose humble homes tower over the miniature tepee prairie, think of what they saw? How much excitement, vicarious heroism, and nostalgic pleasure did the spectacle provide? And what impression did the prisonlike tenements make on these Native Americans, as they performed with a frenzy that was as unnatural to them as to their bemused

spectators? Were they duly moved by "civilization and enlightenment"? Did they wonder who was civilized and who was imprisoned?

These twentieth-century anachronisms found their best representation in the United States. The New World had long promised an exceptional opportunity to relive an earlier moment in human history—a contemporaneous Stone Age on the American frontier. But by 1906, just when the United States began entering the world stage as a serious player, this promise had lost its plausibility. The last major "battle" against Indians at Wounded Knee occurred in 1890; federal land grants were terminated around the same time. Now came the conviction that the "noble savages"—and the old promise of the frontier—required special measures to preserve. To enclose, to display, and to remember—such impulses shaped the birth of the twentieth century, as a heightened sense of the inexorable march of time increasingly mingled with desperate attempts to stop the flow of time, or at least temporarily arrest it for a pleasant moment from the spectator's seat.

So sit awhile and gaze comfortably on these distant "savages." Recall how the progress of this century has provided quiet moments of confident leisure, but take time to appreciate the strangeness and sameness in the varieties of human life and to indulge in that juxtaposition of cultures and creeds that the twentieth century has made its own.

Kevin M. Doak

First Car

There they are gawking at the slick machine, with the shiny headlights and side boards and the plush leather upholstery. The machine seems so incomparably more powerful than the horses, donkeys and camels used for conveyance by people of different stations in town now. Imagine the comfort and ease with which the automobile could take you to the edge of town, or to the boats by the river landing. Imagine what the sublime Mademoiselle de Laurent would say if I offered to take her for a spin, down Boulevard St. Germain, passing by all the sidewalk cafés filled with people, looking. . . . But the daring of this here driver! To have come in the automobile from the port, crossing the mountains, braving the muddy tracks that pass for roads, fighting for the right-of-way with the riders and the carriages. We know how dangerous this cross-country motoring is: The car stalls, the brakes fail, the carburetor malfunctions, one misses a curve, hits a fence or a cart in the road. It is dangerous to be conveyed across country—without rails for guidance—at thirty-five miles an hour!

Between the 1890s and 1930s most of our grandparents or great-grandparents had their first encounter with the automobile, in cities and villages on every continent, from Kansas to the Khyber Pass, and from Mérida to Monrovia. This encounter sparked popular dreams and imaginings almost instantly: dreams of adventure and freedom, but also of enhanced leisure and comfort. With more than 800 million automobiles built worldwide in the past century, the car has blurred the divide for comfortable, rapid transportation between elites and the masses that was once so marked in world history. The automobile age has also fundamentally transformed countrysides and cityscapes, reworked the economies of nation states, and re-assembled global civilization.

By the late 1890s magazines were filled with cartoons showing the recklessness of speeding motorists, goggled eyes fixed on the rutted path, without regard for obstacles. Advertisements selling everything from cigarettes to bread portrayed strutting young motor racers. And from the beginning there has been an association of the sleek machines with beauty, sexual desire, and male prowess. American courting rituals began to move "from the front porch to the back seat" decades before drive-in movie theaters became popular in the 1950s. The automobile also transformed family life, from shopping to the summer vacation. As early as the mid-1920s, the Lynds reported in their famous study of "Middletown," housewives would sooner economize on food than give up their automobile.

Beyond these private dreams the endless transformations that the automobile wrought on life around the globe seemed to take on a life of their own, out of control of the citizens, steered by forces and interests too powerful for them to shape. From the 1910s to the 1980s the automobile and its offshoots, such as the omnibus, the truck, and the tractor, became the most dynamic sector of industrial economies, leading to the rise of new manufacturing centers, directly or indirectly employing as much as one-fifth of national labor forces, and exerting a decisive influence on the business cycle. Even "underdeveloped" economies underwent massive change through motor transport, as isolated rural regions suddenly were flooded with cheaper industrial goods trucked in, and the peasants saw opportunities to send their crops to distant markets. Around the globe motor transport pushed the explosive growth of conurbanizations of unprecedented size, as much through the urban flight of affluent middle classes to suburbs planned around the automobile as through the mushrooming of helter-skelter shantytowns of rural migrants dumped in the cities by buses and trucks. By the mid-twentieth century automobile and petroleum companies headed the Fortune 500 list of the largest global corporations, and theories of development described states with mature economies as ones of mass consumption and the automobile. Automobile companies had little difficulty insisting that their interests coincided with those of the public.

The beckon of the open road and prosperity seemed to go hand-in-hand. It has only been an afterthought that the private automobile dreams of freedom and comfort may also be related to the public nightmares of urban sprawl, the decay of inner cities, and the degradation of the environment.

Nils P. Jacobsen

Bridges

In a century distinguished by ever-increasing velocities of movement, by instant communications amongst once-isolated peoples, by the atrophying of space around an earth grown small, few metaphors are more apt for the twentieth century than the simple bridge. The technology of the bridge in its modern form owes little to the twentieth century beyond the use of reinforced concrete, but our hurried passages across these bridges and our attachment of special meaning to them are an important part of the twentieth-century story. What they have become is summarized in juxtaposing Roebling's first suspension bridge at Wheeling, West Virginia (1846), against the fame and beauty of the majestic suspension span that is synonymous with that engineering technique, the Golden Gate, symbol of both San Francisco and America's entry among Pacific nations, built ninety years later.

What made the bridge a quintessential technological symbol of the twentieth century was the internal combustion engine. The rise of a motoring public required a quantum leap in the construction of bridges, formerly built primarily to accommodate rail networks. During the twentieth century they became heavy-laden political symbols, too. In wartime their destruction and their capture in battle became marks of military prowess. Their site, as a no-man's-land, for negotiations in peacetime celebrates their neutrality, an in-betweenness that is simultaneously

safe and precarious. And this may explain their being a favored, private place for self-destruction, a silent, isolated, structural limbo where no one tarries.

During the preceding century the great public monuments to human mobility in the age of steam were rail terminals. Thanks to the car, bridges took their place in that iconography of travel during the first half of the twentieth century, just as airport terminals succeeded bridges during the last half of the century. The greatest of them incorporate the ultimate twentieth-century Sisyphean political simile for problems that may be incapable of solution, despite the solution apparently always in sight, as painters complete their job at one end of the structure to

travel to the opposite side to begin painting anew.

The suspension bridge pictured here was completed in 1974 and spans the Bosphorous at Istanbul. Straight ahead, a ferryboat will carry you across the Black Sea into southern Ukraine. Moving laterally, across the bridge, is the only road link between the Asian landmass and Europe, providing a twenty-minute drive across a divide that armies and religions on the two continents have contested for millennia. On the right is Asia; New Delhi is perhaps six days of hard driving away (politics being cooperative and bridges open). On the left is Europe, Edinburgh is perhaps five days' drive (politics being cooperative and bridges open). Few sites on the globe demonstrate more perfectly humankind's quest for and achievement of connection in the twentieth century. And at the same time few sites on the globe illustrate so well the fragility of our global connections as this single thin thread of wire and concrete.

Charles C. Stewart

History of the Future

At the end of the twentieth century the mushroom cloud has lost the power to evoke dread. What had been a terrifying possibility for almost half a century has turned out to be a future unrealized, a future past. Looking at the images of nuclear tests, such as this off the Bikini Islands in 1946, viewers today are not drawn in by the reality of horror; they are taken aback by its surreal quality: gently waving palms beneath man's most destructive force. Instead of an alarming example of what is possible, the familiar picture of the mushroom cloud is a fading specter of a twentieth-century future that no longer hangs over the globe.

The twentieth century is distinctive for fashioning a series of completely different futures, each anachronistic and juxtaposed upon the others. The various generations that have grown up in the years since 1900 are at odds with one another precisely because each one grew up holding very idiosyncratic ideas about the goodness of humankind, the benefits of technology, the cultural capacity of democratic societies, and the possibility of global apocalypse.

What do the ruins of the twentieth century look like? The first future was bold, confident, and basically untroubled about the course of history. Around 1900, at least in Europe and the Americas, most commentators assumed that the twentieth century would follow the itinerary laid out by the nineteenth century: the Great Powers (Britain, France, Germany, Austria, and Russia) would remain the main actors on the world stage; political and social institutions would sustain the moral development of citizens; and technology would assure ever greater economic prosperity and rational control of the environment.

World War I gloomed up this bright future. The long war itself, the revolutions and dictatorships that followed, and the harsh economics of hyperinflation and the Great Depression created a divide that forever separated the hopeful, steady future of the pre-1914 years from the turbulence of the postwar years. Millions of dead fathers and sons and many more millions of crippled veterans and displaced refugees told of the unimagined violence of the twentieth century. Never before had the material edifices of civilization seemed so fragile. Yet this extreme jeopardy also indicated the ease with which social structures might be reconfigured. It is not surprising that during the postwar years Communists and Fascists busily planned the coming twentieth-century future, each imagining very different societies but both to be imposed by the wartime mobilization of men and materiel. And both ideological contestants assumed that the birth of the new order would be violent. After World War I, the future was premised on discontinuity.

The rise of global military blocks, promiscuous developments in technology and science, and the rapid extension of the world market continued to rework the face of the globe after World War II. The post-1945 future appeared increasingly uniform, if still scary. Frightful images of wartime destruction were focused on the single riveting image of the final atomic blast. The workings of mass society gave critics in Europe and the Third World frightening images of an homogenized world in which standards of taste, refinement, and intellect had no place. If the post–World War I era had indicated the hazards to life posed by machines, the post–World War II years raised the possibility of life as a machine.

At the very end of the century, however, given the collapse of the Soviet Union and the end of the cold war, the future looks terrifying open-ended. Citizens share neither the pre-1914 faith in science nor the post-1914 commitment to ideology. What does appear menacing today is not the effacement of cultural traits by technology but the renewed pronunciation of ethnic and religious differences. In a world in which neither progress nor catastrophe, neither the promise of nuclear engineering nor the dread of nuclear warfare, looms on the horizon, the future tense is no longer as useful or imperative. The wave of the future may have passed.

Peter Fritzsche

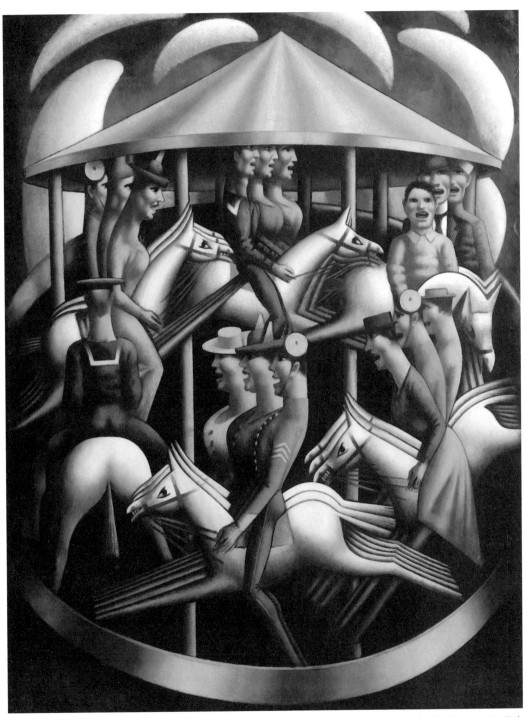

22

The Merry-Go-Round

Ordinarily a merry-go-round evokes an image of childhood and playtime, of county fairs and amusement parks. But the open-mouthed mechanical figures in this painting by Mark Gertler conjure up a far more ominous theme.

Even in the earliest decades of modern industry, social critics such as William Blake had denounced the "dark Satanic mills" in which women and children slaved side-by-side during twelve-hour days in textile factories, each tending identical spinning machines bound to a single source of power, a giant steam engine. The total amount of human drudgery may have been far greater during the pre-industrial era, but social critics from Karl Marx to Charlie Chaplin were appalled by the deadening and dehumanizing quality of the mechanical assembly line in which human beings had apparently become no more than interchangeable cogs in a gigantic industrial wheel.

When World War I began in 1914, many volunteer soldiers were attracted to the romantic notion that armed conflict would give them the chance to win personal glory, and that war was itself the ultimate amusement-park shooting gallery. Within a few months, disillusion began to set in. The trenches of the western front became mired in mud and repetitive exchanges of machine-gun fire. The stalemate that ensued swallowed up an apparently unending supply of both volunteers and conscripts. Gertler's painting therefore evokes a hellish vision of humankind transformed into a vicious circle of shouting manic automata.

Born in 1891, Mark Gertler was the son of Jewish immigrants who had recently moved from the Austro-Hungarian Empire to London's East End. There he grew up in dire poverty until talent spotters of the Jewish Educational Aid Society sent him to the Slade School of Art, where he became a prize pupil. Eventually, he became associated with the Bloomsbury group, that gathering of writers, painters, and critics (Virginia Woolf and Lytton Strachey among them) who sought to debunk the standards and mores of their Victorian parents. Yet the pre-1914 concerns of such self-professed liberators began to seem trivial in the face of a continent-wide specter of obedient citizens tethered to the mechanical spokes of a totally mobilized warrior state.

Gertler survived the war as an apparently successful studio painter, but his vision of the twentieth century remained disturbed. On the eve of World War II, he took his own life.

Walter L. Arnstein

Disillusion

Ullstein Bilderdienst

When European armies mobilized in the summer of 1914, war was still regarded as a glorious undertaking. A generation marched off, much like these German troops in Berlin, cheered by light-hearted crowds who believed their cause just and their soldiers invincible. But the vicious realities of war in the industrial age quickly crushed their enthusiasm. Europeans came to mistrust the easy verse of patriotism. They found their faith in human progress misplaced. Science and technology, which had always been associated with prosperous and enlightened well-being, seemed to connive against the men in the trenches, who were mown down by machine guns, torn apart by artillery, and suffocated by poison gas. Soldiers had become mere ciphers in a vast technological conflict. Stumbling, shuffling, terrorized lines of casualties such as these gas-blinded British Tommies replaced the spirited parades at the war's outset.

This was not the first war to shatter illusions, but the exigencies of mass mobilization and the confidence of the Belle Epoque in science and technology combined to devastate Europeans. States mustered armies far larger than had ever taken the field before. States also reached deep into the civilian population to find workers and volunteers. As in earlier conflicts, men in the field and their families back home learned lessons of suffering and futility, but the numbers of men and women involved were now extraordinary. War moved entire populations, from home into factory, from civilian purposes to martial

25

pursuits, from casual days to vigilant nights.

In 1914, the Continent was also woefully ignorant of war's fundamentally brutal nature. Europeans had not suffered a general continental war since 1815, and the conflicts of the mid-nineteenth century, such as the Austro-Prussian War, had been deceptively brief and decisive. As a result the experience of war was basically literary and largely mythologized. Technology had also given the West such an overwhelming advantage in colonial conflicts that great victories could be had easily and fine heroes could still find a role. As a result, the disillusionment of the years 1914–18 was extreme, and gave way to a broad social disorientation that found its literary voice in the famously "lost" generation of Fitzgerald and Hemingway.

The twentieth century really began with World War I, which shattered expectations of a better future and shredded confidence in the means and ends of European history. The experience of the war was so forceful that Europeans considered the peace merely an interlude before a more titanic struggle. Both the Soviet Union and Nazi Germany renovated themselves as gigantic armories of state power. In World War II, all-out mobilization turned horribly genocidal. And the atomic bomb realized the worst fears of the long-range bombing that had been current since Germany's zeppelin raids over London in 1915. The Great War pulled the shadow of war across the twentieth century.

John A. Lynn

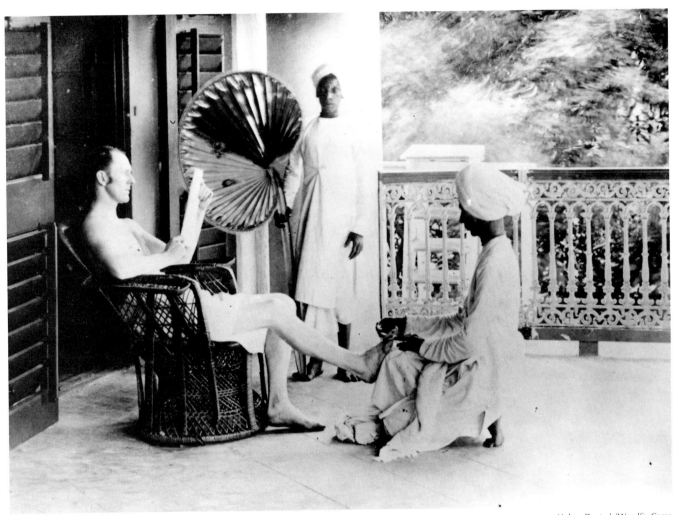

Imperialism

"A well-trained cook is nearly equal to any European chef, but back home you can never find a man-servant to equal the chaps I have had in my service."

"Our object is nothing less than the transportation of these peoples into the mainstream of the twentieth century."

"In my many years of service for the Crown in India, then Sudan, Nigeria and Gambia, I will have to admit that I never met a native I didn't like and who wouldn't respond well to bit of cash or a boot to the backside."

"It may take a century or more to truly civilize these people."

"What they need to learn are the rewards of good, honest work; sweat and toil with something tangible at the other end like a crop to export or a pay envelope."

"Thanks to the work of the Christian fathers, who in so many ways have been the handmaiden of our work in these parts, I know I have seen a change for the better in the mentality of these people in the twenty-five years I have served the Empire."

"It is not their evident enjoyment at the competition of football games that disturbs me (although we really must watch this), but it is their demands that they be allowed to wear shoes while playing the game that strikes at the very foundation of our relationship with the native."

"The religion of these people may be one of their most debilitating (and certainly one of their most time-consuming) customs, but it is thanks to the help of their religious leaders that our work here has been greatly facilitated."

"It is with regret that the Military Pension Fund cannot honor its commitment to compensation for the mutilation and lives lost of colonial subjects who present multiple wives as beneficiaries, since such benefits may be subject to falsification and the Fund is foremost responsible for the loss of European lives."

"To make the native proud to serve the Empire is one of the most fundamental challenges to our educational system."

"The purpose of taxation, after all, is not revenue, however helpful that may be for minor projects. The purpose of our taxation system is forcing the native into doing a day's work and learning the value, indeed, the civilizing influence of hard labor."

"Unofficially, it is recognized that officers may take a local woman for limited periods of time, but utmost care must be exerted to avoid unnecessary relationships and under no circumstances may such a person be transferred to the officer's new posting."

"Yes, there may have been some overzealous officers and a few unnecessary deaths in the course of our development of ports and railways, but I have never heard a native complain about his ability to purchase the latest Manchester fabrics brought through those ports and by that rail."

"The dangerous ones are the ones who have just begun to read but have not yet realized the advantages our Empire offers to he who stays in the system. They're really like children."

Charles C. Stewart

Lenin's Light Bulb

The socialist *idea* was a child of the nineteenth century, a reaction to economic and social inequality, a solution to the incomplete promise of liberty left over from the French Revolution. Socialist *practice* was the progeny of the twentieth century, as Russia became the first country in the world to create a socialist system. The promise of socialism was attractive: public ownership of a country's economic assets could create huge surpluses to benefit society as a whole. But the challenge of socialism in Russia was how to create a modern industrial economy in a sprawling multiethnic country made up mostly of semiliterate peasants. Vladimir Ilyich Lenin crafted the slogan that would meet the challenge: "Communism equals Soviet power plus the electrification of the entire country." The soviets (councils) represented revolutionary democracy. Electrification symbolized the technological leap forward that would transform the economy, creating abundance where under the old regime there had only been poverty. Gigantic hydroelectric dams would power steel mills, chemical plants, and machine factories. Eventually such investments would finance consumer goods and social services to make life easier for all.

Just as important as material well-being was the cultural transformation that socialism would make in the lives of ordinary citizens. Socialist industrialization would become possible only by raising the cultural level of the So-viet people; but industrialization would also make possible this cultural development. "Lenin's light bulbs," fired by the new electrical plants, would bring light and enlightenment to the dark villages of the Russian expanse. In this photograph, the young man from the city—the herald of socialism—demonstrates to the old peasant woman just how electricity could enrich her life. The light bulb stood for the economic and cultural modernization that Communism would advance.

One of the proudest victories of the Soviet regime was the achievement of universal literacy in a country that spanned one-sixth of the globe, but this and other accomplishments of the socialist order—the victory over Germany, the attainment of superpower status in the 1950s and beyond—came at untold costs. By the end of the twentieth century, it was evident that the socialist economic method of central planning had produced not an economy of untold abundance but an economy of perpetual shortages. One of the best indicators of this deficit economy was the black market in *burned-out* light bulbs. It was almost impossible to buy light bulbs by the late 1980s. So consumers simply removed bulbs from public places (stairwells, offices, wherever they could) and replaced them with worn-out bulbs bought on the black market, to cover up their autonomous redistribution of socialist property.

Diane P. Koenker

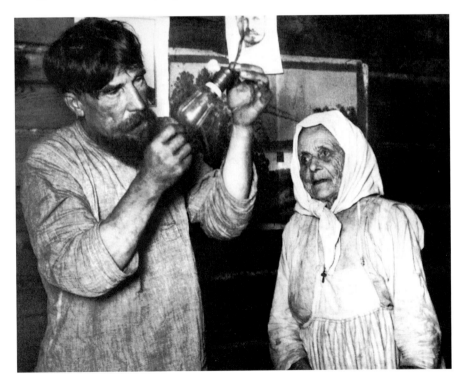

Jersey Shore

Three young women. Swimsuits. Seashore. Cigarettes. Staged for the camera. This photo from the "Roaring Twenties" is a powerful visual image of modernity. It evokes fantasy, fun, and female independence. These are three "New Women" who partake of the pleasures of twentieth-century mass production and the new leisure possibilities. Apparently they are unburdened by chaperones, husbands, or children; the picture speaks of a new age. Working in factories, offices, and as salesgirls, women of the 1920s could afford the luxuries of ready-to-wear clothing, trips to the boardwalk and beach, and cigarettes.

These women wear extremely short and revealing clothing—a startling contrast to the lengthy, heavy skirts of the nineteenth century—and show bare, shaven legs. Almost at the very center of the picture are the cigarettes, symbols of indulgence and independence. Whereas smoking had been a highly masculine habit, and off-limits to women, cigarette manufacturers now promoted the equation of smoking with female liberty.

At the very moment that American women won the right to vote, advertisers told them that freedom in the twentieth century meant the right to consume.

Leslie J. Reagan

Keystone-Mast Collection, UCR/California Museum of Photography, Neg.#KU86083

Gandhi

In the early morning of April 6, 1931, after a march to the seashore of twenty-four days, Mahatma Gandhi bent over and picked up a handful of salt and with that simple act shook the power of the British Indian Empire. He had challenged the government monopoly on the manufacture and sale of salt which inflicted a heavy tax on a necessity of life for the poorest Indians. Thousands followed his example and soon all over India there were carefully planned civil disobedience campaigns led by Gandhi's lieutenants.

Gandhi's *satyagraha* or "soul force" campaigns inspired a new, peculiarly twentieth-century type of political action—unarmed citizens standing fast on moral issues and defying mighty governments. From Gandhi's example came the civil disobedience campaigns of the sixties, seventies, and eighties that empowered ordinary citizens to face police truncheons with courage and equanimity—in America the civil rights movement of Martin Luther King, the anti–Vietnam War movement, and the women's rights movement; in the Soviet Union and Eastern Europe the defiance of "refusniks" and dissidents; and everywhere in the world the environmental and antinuclear movements.

Of the dozens of *satyagraha* campaigns launched by Gandhi, the salt march was the most successful and proved to skeptics everywhere the power of Gandhi's unconventional method. In salt Gandhi had discovered a powerful symbol, a common household item of special concern to women and the poor. Even many British recognized the absurdity of a law prohibiting poor peasants from gathering salt from the seashore. The actual march was a matter of two hundred miles, but it became a symbol for later civil disobedience movements—part crusade, part pilgrimage, mass action at once peaceful and threatening.

The salt march captured the imagination of people in Europe and America; newspaper reporters and camera crews came from everywhere; and the attention of the entire world was focused on the small man in the shawl and his humble group of followers. The government was paralyzed—to arrest Gandhi at this moment would bring down the ridicule of the world, to let him continue meant abdicating their duty to uphold the laws of the land. This particular civil disobedience movement marked the beginning of the end of British rule in India. While most other colonial governments eventually fell to armed revolt, the British Indian Empire was mortally wounded by a handful of salt.

Blair B. Kling

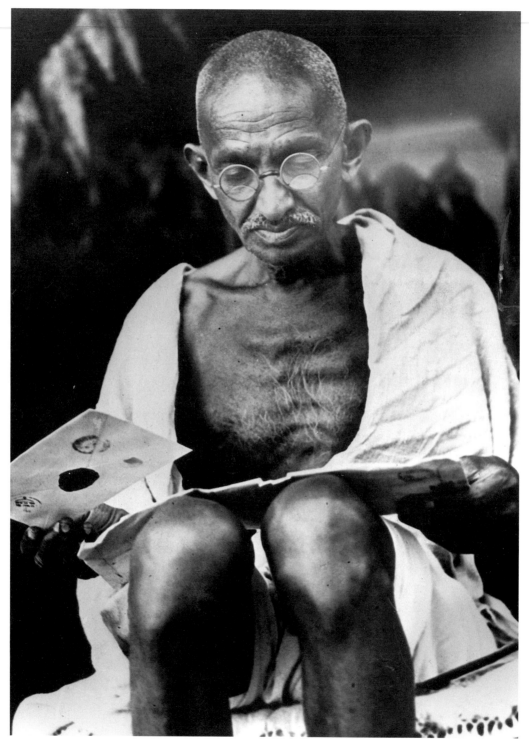

33

Music

Our age is one of persistent, relentless, almost unbearable inquiry. In its exaltation it cuts off all retreats and bans all sanctuaries; its passion is contagious, its thirst for the unknown projects us forcefully, violently into the future.... Despite the skillful ruses we have cultivated in our desperate effort to make the world of the past serve our present needs, we can no longer elude the essential trial: that of becoming an absolute part of the present, of forsaking all memory to forge a perception without a precedent, of renouncing the legacies of the past, to discover yet undreamed-of territories.

Political vision? Credo for the postmodern age? Declaration of the end of history? Pierre Boulez spoke these words at the opening of the French Institut de Recherche et de Coordination Acoustique/Musique in the mid-1970s.

No century of music has sounded such change and transformation as has the twentieth. It was the first time music has been written and performed for no live audience; the first time players have listened to and compared each other's full repertoire; the first time, through dubbing, they have been able to guarantee an unflawed performance; the first time compositions have been written expressly for electronic instruments that no individual is capable of performing; the first large-scale importation of non-Western musics into

European and North American music cultures.

In the West the century opened with the pastel tones of post-Romanticism and impressionists like Debussy and Ravel, soon rivaled by the eclecticism, unpredictable rhythms, contrasts, and bold colors of neoclassicists Stravinsky and Hindemith, Bartók and Prokofiev, and the hyperintellectual dodecaphony expressionism of Hartmann. As elsewhere in the world of theater, film, and fine arts, these composers and artists sought to celebrate the exotic "other" as global cultures drew together and to give sound to their expressions and reactions to the machine age. In Debussy's words, "The century of the aeroplane deserves its music."

But in one of those ironies that define the century, particular artifacts of that machine age were to act on the production of music more-so than music was to chronicle production itself. The phonograph and, after World War II, the tape recorder and synthe-

"Embrace," Herbert Brün, shape sequence 2

34

sizer revolutionized performance. They made for instant access to other performers' work and made accessible rare instrumentation and musics from the non-Western world. Performers' reputations as recording artists came to determine their drawing power in concert. Composition, as had earlier occurred with the venerable piano roll, could be directed expressly by the technology. The influence of sound recordings was to turn music journals of the 1930s into reviews of the latest recordings by the 1960s, and catapult recording producers into a position of importance that vied with that of performers themselves.

Dramatic as these changes were, more important still was the expansion of the repertoire of sonic resources, synthesized sounds, and recordings of sounds in nature—all contributing to what Russolo termed "the art of noises." Commenting on his master's legacy, Boulez observed, "[Messiaen] has taught us to look around us and to understand that *all* can become music."

Beneath these developments was an even more fundamental pattern that may be the true twentieth-century mark on our musics: the emergence of a music that was stripped of pitch and melody as distinguishing characteristics, leaving us with rhythm as its organizing principle. The eclecticism, alone, has called on new systems for annotating sounds. And, as *all* became music, notation and designs for musical composition fused computers with creativity, as in Herbert Brün's *Embrace*, reproduced below. For some this means an inchoate diversity. Art music and pop music are increasingly fused, yet

they coexist alongside other genres that stretch back to the beginning of our period. And, at century's end, they make room for works of greater simplicity and a more accessible music in which melody has once again found a place.

Our age is one of persistent, relentless, almost unbearable inquiry.
Charles C. Stewart

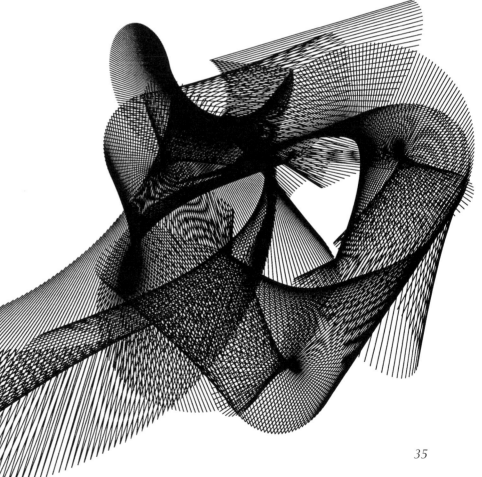

Intolerance

The juxtapositions are familiar and chilling: religion, nationalism, and self-righteous hatred—the cross, the flags, and the ghostly robes of the Ku Klux Klan. In a country that has reason to pride itself on ideals of tolerance and equal opportunity, the mindsets that made this bizarre group picture possible deserve a second look. Today the image of the Klan is either a distant historical echo of the night-riding terrorist of the Reconstruction South or a contemporary caricature of a mar-

ginal fringe of bigoted losers. But in the 1920s when this picture was taken, the so-called Invisible Empire of the Knights of the Ku Klux Klan and its brand of "100% Americanism" was the decade's most potent, influential social movement. At its height, this KKK boasted awesome political muscle. It could make or break political careers as it engineered elections of United States senators, mayors, and legislative majorities from Indiana to Oklahoma, from Alabama to Oregon.

The key to the Klan's success lies in the difficult passage as the United

States shifted to a more mobile, cosmopolitan society. Tumultuous change invited nativist reassertions and cultural backlash. The white, Protestant, native-born Americans who joined the KKK by the millions in the 1920s were—to an extent that may surprise us today—mainstream Americans. They commonly paired suspicions of subversive conspiracies with an intimate sense of community, a mix that the Klan and its rousing rituals of secrecy could provide. Many in the KKK had been alienated not only by "radical" labor unions but by community business and politi-

Collection Dancing Bear

cal elites who blocked popular reforms; one frequent target was the civic corruption that accompanied the failure to enforce the newly enacted national prohibition of liquor. Members were determined, sometimes through violence and intimidation but usually through the electoral process and rallies, to enforce their "traditional" values and their feelings of belonging against Catholics, Jews, immigrants, African Americans, "painted women," Jazz Age libertines, and anyone else who deviated from their vision of pure Americanism. By casting their nation in their own idealized image, Klansmen fashioned an exclusivist American identity whose appeal persists to this day.

From the assassination of Archduke Ferdinand in the future Yugoslavia to the modern ethnic cleansing in the former Yugoslavia, from the bloody riots culminating in the postcolonial partition of India and Pakistan to the Hutu and Tutsi massacres in Rwanda, the global mobilization of ethnic and religious difference has taken an appalling toll. The appeal of such mobilizations reflects the duality of identity politics, both a powerful source of internal cohesion and a threat to those outside. Scholars see nationalism as a product of modernity, closely tied to the rise of modern states and economies; yet they recognize it also as a reaction against that modernity. Although the United States is often seen as the prime exemplar of inclusive, tolerant "civic nationalism," as opposed to more destructive ethnonationalism so prevalent elsewhere, the Klan is a reminder that American "civic nationalism" is a work in progress, scarred by intolerance and frequently under siege.

Mark H. Leff

A Nisei in the Andes

A portrait of a "typical Japanese family" taken in 1941. It tells us much about pride and aspirations, about a sense of propriety and dignity, but also about fears for the future. These people are obviously not wellborn or affluent. But the photo reveals no context, no markers about the environment where the family resided. We might assume that this is a portrait similar to millions of others taken of families in towns and villages across the island archipelago of Japan.

In fact, the picture was taken in a photo studio in Lima, Peru. This is the Fujimori family, part of Peru's Japanese "colony." Driven by rural poverty in their home country, thousands of Japanese families came to make a living, as farmers, workers, shopkeepers, or craftsmen, braving barriers of language, religion, and intolerance. The older boy looking so quizzically into the camera is Alberto, born on a hacienda in the arid Andean piedmont on Peruvian Independence Day, July 28, 1938. On another Peruvian Independence Day, in 1990, Alberto Fujimori would be inaugurated as president of Peru. One of the country's most powerful presidents of this century, he has drawn strength from his popularity among the Andean ("Indian") peasantry. President Fujimori regularly travels to remote hamlets in the Andes, dancing "huaynos" with the members of the community at their fiesta and promising help from Lima for myriad local problems. The Nisei "El Chinito" has become a virtuoso of Peruvian politics.

Migration and cultural hybridity have become a mark of this century. Streams of migrants today are connecting virtually every country. Colonies from the world's larger national or ethnic groups have fanned out to all five continents. By the 1980s even a tiny island nation such as Cape Verde (off the west coast of Africa) had two or three big-city "beach heads" on different sides of "its" ocean. In fact, much of this century's transnational migration has been among non-Western or Third World countries. The Saitos, Okinishis, and Morimotos came from rural Kyushu and Hokkaido to Peru, Brazil, Korea, and northern China in the first half of this century. Since the mid-nineteenth century the Suns, Lifus, and Huangs were violently taken as coolies from Macao and Hong Kong to plantations and railroad construction sites in the Caribbean and Peru, and other Chinese settled in cities around the Pacific and Indian Oceans. Traveling within the British Empire, Mr. Reginder Singh and thousands like him early in the century came from Calcutta to Dar es Salaam, Durban, Guyana, Belize, or Jamaica. Even before the Ottoman Empire came apart in 1919, Mr. Mehir Said and his clan from Aleppo fanned out to commercial entrepôts in both hemispheres and established a finely spun network of shopkeepers and

Eduardo Zegovia/Caretas, Lima #1227

38

traders, from San Pedro de Zula to Santiago de Chile, from Dakar to Cape Town. By the 1930s there was a thriving community of African Brazilians in Lagos, Nigeria. Millions of Filipina women and Bangladeshi, Pakistani, and Indian men flocked to the oil states bordering the Persian Gulf during the 1970s and 1980s. Migrants between neighboring states—from Afghanistan to Pakistan, from Botswana, Zimbabwe, and Mozambique to South Africa, and from Colombia to Venezuela—have been even more numerous.

Most migrants have dreamt ambivalent dreams: "making it" in their new environment, and returning "home" sooner or later, as respected members of their native communities. They plunge into the daily rhythms of their host societies, adapting to unaccustomed rhythms of work, and to strange foods, to the language and to the universe of local meanings it entails. In the communities of migrants from their village, their region, or nation, they reconstruct how things were back home (or how they remember them). Marriages are arranged between the children of two honorable families from the same valley back home; the rituals prescribed for weddings, deaths, and births are adhered to as much as the new setting allows. The migrants seek to ensure that their children will not lose those core meanings of their lives.

The unprecedented scale of migration, especially between non-Western

Caretas, Lima

countries, has forced most denizens of the twentieth century to deal with "foreigners." It has given cultures the world over opportunities to create new rituals, practices, and art forms, by incorporating culture traits brought by the migrants. Such have been major building blocks for an emerging global culture by the century's end.

Nils P. Jacobsen

Typist

No single piece of machinery in the twentieth century has bent so many people into standard shapes by insistently coaxing their fingers, steadily tensing their backs, and prescribing norms in the office as the typewriter. To this day, keyboards structure our thoughts and moderate our communications. Strings of keyboards have also quietly mechanized social interactions in the corporate office. By 1930, twenty-three thousand typing schools had opened in the United States; their exercises are exemplary of the mechanisms of collaboration, a mechanization that has made a distinctively twentieth-century fate.

Peter Fritzsche

Typing habits are shifting, conditioned behavior. As an illustration of conditioning to countless slight signals or cues typewriting is admirably clear cut.

Errors for the Teacher to Check

Touch too heavy
Touch too light
Touch too sluggish
Touch uneven
Body not square in front of
    typewriter—too far left or right
Body too close or too far from
    typewriter
Body twisted
Body humped over
Head bent
Spine bent
Body too tense
Feet sprawled widely
Feet twisted under chair
Feet on braces of desk
Elbows akimbo
Wrists sagging
Wrists too high, wrists too stiff
Looking at fingers
Looking up at end of line
Looking at distractions

One hand waits for the other. There is no excuse for it. . . . Now I think she ought to dive for her paper, and not wait for the other hand. She should bend all energies on the piece of paper that is going up. (From Gilbreth's *Motion-Study Notes*)

During his typewriting, Scott's machine developed a mechanical defect which made it impossible to print the capitals. Isn't such irritating interference enough to bring a real body upset? Note the clues with which Scott groped for a way out of his keenly felt difficulty. First, however, he defined the problem by noting that the ribbon carrier would not lift to meet the type when the shift key was used. Starting with the obvious causal relation between pressing a key and the lifting of the ribbon carrier, Scott inferred that something had become unhooked or loosened, somewhere between key and ribbon carrier. He traced the complicated mechanical relationships of his typewriter by a transfer of ideas from his experience, such ideas as "I must proceed in a systematic way," "friction will produce wearing," "directions of force when inclined planes are brought

together in various ways," "actions of springs," "levers," and "machines work as units." After two hours of this careful experimenting, testing out this clue and rejecting that, the source of the trouble emerged. With the completeness of his new idea of just what to do went a new insight into this sort of difficulty. The tension relaxed. The typewriter resumed its leisurely clicking.

By the twenty-third day, I was still reaching to individual keys as such, but more quickly. My hands and fingers were clearly becoming more flexible and adept. The change then going on, aside from growing flexibility, was in learning to locate keys without waiting to see them, in other words, to find keys by position. The boredom recently so noticeable was disappearing. The feeling of pleasure which colored the beginning of the work returned. (A student's diary entry)

Percentages of Girls of Various Ages Who Report That They Would "Like Best" to Be (a) Stenographers or Typists, (b) Movie Actresses [1929]

Age in Years	Typists	Movie Actresses
10½	14%	29%
12½	26%	17%
14½	31%	10%
16½	32%	5%

Preoccupation with pulchritude on the part of the employer may not be noble and high-minded, but it is a fact. It's sex. You can't fight it. But you might develop a few slogans to put over your more exciting products, such as, "Here's Holyoke's Hottest—Handle with Asbestos Gloves" . . . or, "Smith Girls are Girlier Girls."

Are you out of line somehow in the typing class? Is it becoming a hardship to conform with the everyday requirements for "standard" typists and future secretaries? It is usually taken for granted that you will follow the expected ways. If you venture to try a new and different way, you may disturb your associates to an extent that startles you.

Freud

In this century, the great promise that the triumph of reason would be achieved has faced formidable foes who have held that rational thinking is permanently blocked by the mysterious, the instinctual, the subjective. The clash between the forces of reason and unreason gave special power to modernist anxieties about the progress of civilization, and it opened the door for a Viennese physician, Sigmund Freud (1856–1939), to develop a therapy and a worldview that would square the circle of the modern age: Freud applied science to the heart of the unknowable, linking the ego, the unconscious, and the sex drive.

Seeking to treat the mysterious class of ailments classified as neurasthenia, Freud argued that neurosis was explained by circumstantial factors, which could be best understood by exploring infantile sexuality. From here he developed an elaborate theory that used childhood memories, dreams, fantasies, slips of the tongue, and witticisms to diagnose nervous disorders. Freudian enthusiasts quickly embraced his theory of psychoanalysis and some have continued to apply his methods to the treatment of neurosis.

Freud's method, more linguistic than physiological, has generated tremendous controversy, and strong partisans on both sides defend and denounce his approach. His theory allows for no possibility of scientific proof, but the power of his ideas has generated significant influence for "applied Freudianism." Freud himself pioneered the application of his theories to the realm of human endeavor, extending his investigations to art criticism (in a biography of Leonardo da Vinci based on the painter's chronicle of a dream); to religion; to anthropology; and to civilization itself. In *Totem and Taboo* (1918), Freud applied his analysis of dreams and fantasies to the creation of myths and fairy tales, equating the production of racial myths with the regression to infantile fantasies he observed in his patients. *Civilization and Its Discontents* (1930) might be taken as a charter for the twentieth century, where Freud argues that civilization leads humans to repress their basic instincts, resulting in unhappiness and despair. There is no choice, there is no happy ending. Freud wrote this work when the stern regime of Fascism was already triumphant in Italy, and on the rise in Germany and Austria, his home. Nazi hostility to the Jews would force Freud to pack his shelves of scientific treatises and his collection of primitive artifacts and to leave his Vienna apartment in 1939, on the eve of his death.

Despite the controversy surrounding Freud's scientific method, the world of arts and letters hastened to apply his methods to their own creations. Think of Laurence Olivier's *Hamlet*, with the camera's long slow gaze to the bed of Hamlet's mother. Imagine talking about love without talking about libido, envy, or castration. At the century's end, the passion generated about Freud, both pro and con, was so strong that the Library of Congress found itself in the center of a firestorm when it organized an exhibition on the doctor's life and works. Regardless of Freud's scientific merit, his "clichés of the couch" have become a basic component of the language of the twentieth century, whether in medicine, the arts, philosophy, or popular culture.

Diane P. Koenker

The Crowd

The source of our century's greatest cultural and political upheavals is found not among famous artists and statesman but in the anonymity of faceless crowds. From the birth of Communism in the Russian (1917) and Chinese (1949) Revolutions to its death in Eastern Europe and elsewhere at century's end; from Berlin's 1936 Olympics to the high point of the post-war youth culture at Woodstock (1969), the crowd became a global declaration of mass engagement with political agendas. The crowd can also mix culture with politics as does the one pictured here in the streets of Paris in 1968, which represents a combination of carnival and revolution. Its composition, function, and image have varied across time and space, but the crowd was always there. Why?

The crowd's significance derives largely from the mass character of twentieth-century political ideologies and cultural forms—socialist and fascist movements which displayed their strength as much in the streets as at the polls; the soccer match, rock concert, and other spectator events which live and die with their audiences. Workers, peasants, and students far from the levers of state power have embraced mass protests—land seizures, strikes, sit-ins—as their only obvious political options.

Is the crowd's significance receding at the end of our century? With the dispersion of television, computers, videos, and compact disks, do we experience mass culture more often now as individuals than as crowds? Symbolic, media-based forms of politics have displaced participatory democracy and large-scale protests, while the institutionalization and decline of organized labor has also diminished the crowd's political role. Yet the exceptions to these tendencies are numerous even in the West. Crowds killed the British poll tax in the 1980s, and they enforced the 1995 French strikes against budget cuts, bringing public services and transportation to a halt. In Asia, the Middle East, Africa, and Latin America, the crowd remains a prime mover, even in the face of massive force. In Teheran, where crowds helped to create and then enforce the authority of Islam, among the young people in Peking's Tiananmen Square, and in the South African democracy struggle, crowds exerted enormous political pressure at home and caught the world's attention. Recently, cultural and political explosions have been set off by the fuse of modern communications technology—the Ayatollah's cassette sermons or the faxes radiating around the world from China's democracy movement.

Perhaps there is something more fundamental going on in the crowd than simply performance or politics. As the crowd gathers, Elias Canetti writes, "Suddenly it is as though everything were happening in one and the same body . . . all are equal there, . . . no distinctions count." Perhaps the crowd remains a refuge from the alienation of individualism and in it we continue to sense not only collective power but also the essence of our common humanity.

James R. Barrett

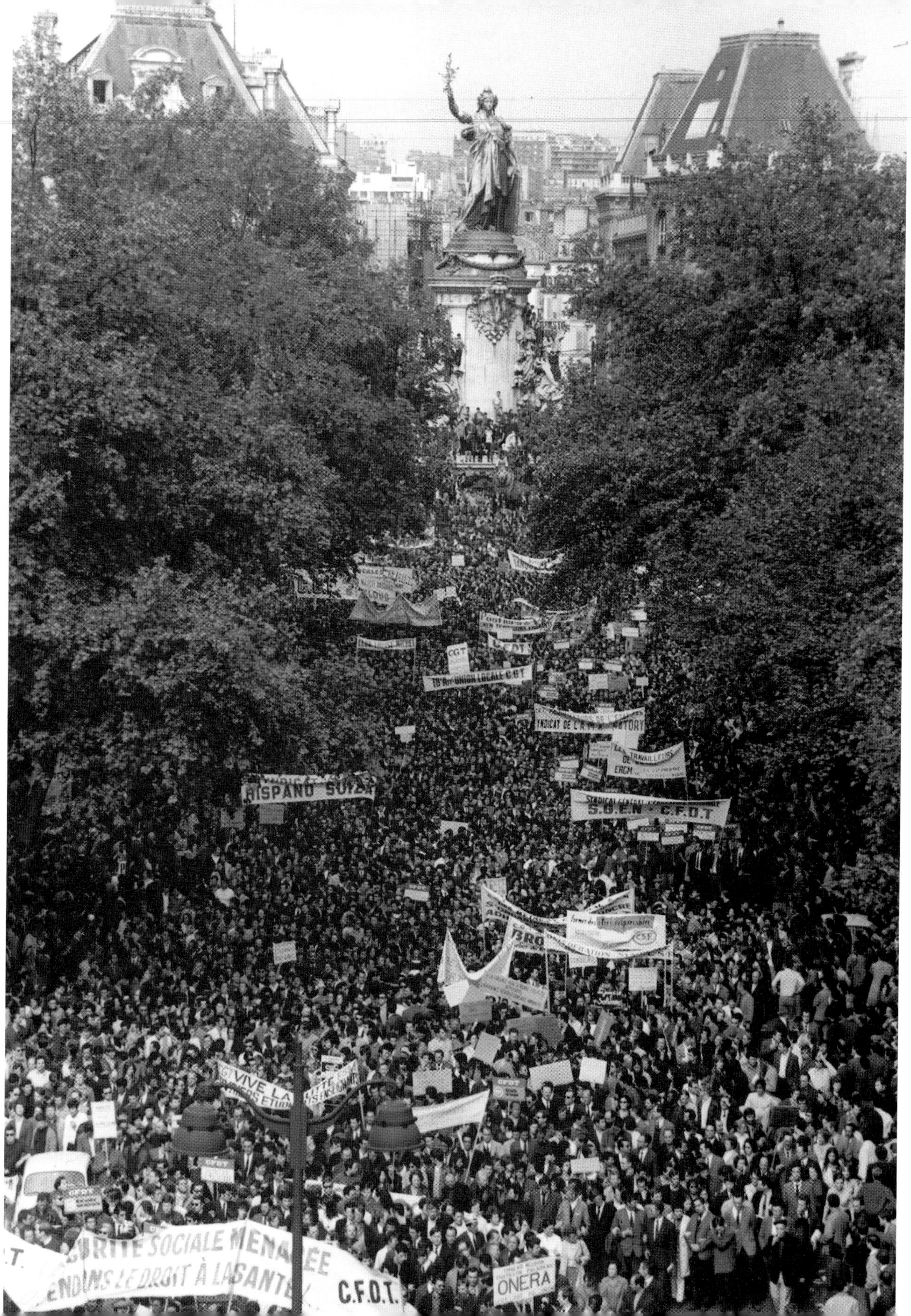

Guy Le Querrec / Magnum Photos

Alfonso, Madrid

The Spanish Civil War

The revolutionary euphoria following the Bolsheviks' 1917 triumph in Russia led many to expect an international upheaval. Instead, a period of political reaction set in, culminating in the rise of fascism, first in Italy in the early 1920s and within a decade in Germany and other parts of Europe. The Communist International predicted in 1935 a cataclysmic conflict between the forces of fascism and democracy and urged revolutionaries of the world to create "Popular Fronts" with any parties willing to oppose the rising fascist tide. The first great engagement of this struggle began in Spain in July 1936, when the military and right-wing political parties, aided by Fascist Italy and Nazi Germany, rose to crush Spain's legally elected Popular Front government with its promises of universal secularized public education, labor laws, and land reform.

On November 7, 1936, the young Spanish Republic seemed destined for a violent death at the hands of its own mutinous military. The Nationalist forces, with backing from the army, large landowners, and the church, had quickly overrun much of the country and were now about to seize the seat of government, Madrid. As the city's citizens prepared for a final defense, a column of two thousand fresh soldiers marched up the Gran Via toward the front. In the fighting that ensued, a total of forty thousand men and women from fifty-two countries around the world joined these International Brigades, including the twenty-eight hundred Americans who formed the Abraham Lincoln Brigade, to defend the Popular Front.

Most of the men and women of the International Brigades were Communists, many of whom had fled repression in their own countries, but they counted among their combatants and supporters people representing a wide spectrum of political thought and some of the most important artists and intellectuals of the interwar generation. The Communists' moral position was vastly strengthened in the course of the thirties by Soviet support for antifascist movements in Spain and elsewhere, while the western democracies followed a policy of nonintervention to avoid a new world war. Spain became a metaphor for the defense of democracy, a measure of political commitment for the twentieth-century Left.

Neither the defeat of the Spanish Republic nor the Nazi-Soviet Non-Aggression Pact in 1939 tarnished the luster of this cause. Leftists employed popular front principles throughout the world in the wake of World War II, creating mass movements ranging from electoral coalitions to anticolonial guerrilla armies. The contest in the political mainstream shifted from one between conservatives and liberals to a new terrain with traditional liberals facing off against the broad Left envisioned in the Popular Front. Out of the Spanish struggle sprang a new kind of political engagement and a new kind of response to pragmatic international politics, the people's cause.

James R. Barrett

No Work

"Unemployment"—soup kitchens, hoboes, protest marches. Images of the Great Depression of the 1930s spring quickly to mind, defining not only a turning point in the century's economic and political history but a generational divide between those who faced poverty and insecurity followed by war and those who grew up amidst plenty. The social dimensions of the event are enormous, and its significance was realized in the personal lives of millions of individuals. This personal experience, captured in the faces pictured here, was one not of anger but bewilderment and what George Orwell called a "haunted . . . feeling of personal degeneration."

We have lived with cyclical and seasonal unemployment throughout our century. A perennial fact of working-class life, more recently it has become a growing concern even among professional and technical elites. Linked by definition to the development of industrial capitalism, unemployment spread with industrialization to the Third World in the past generation and, along with the market, to postcommunist societies in the past decade. Even long-term, structural unemployment, associated in our era with global competition and the decline of manufacturing in western societies, predated the depression. In the 1920s new fuels and fabrics, higher productivity, manufacturing in India and China, and an occupational shift from heavy industry toward service and clerical work all brought permanent decline to coal mining and textile towns throughout northern England, the northeastern United States, and parts of Germany.

Yet there is still something different about the unemployment of the thirties. The numbers alone are staggering. In the United States unemployment jumped from less than one-half million in October 1929 to more than fifteen million—a third of the nation's workforce—four years later. Figures for most Western European countries ran between 20 and 30 percent during the early 1930s. Families lived in packing crates in Chicago's Loop, in abandoned coke ovens in the Pennsylvania coal fields, in caves in Central Park. "Society," the critic Alfred Kazin wrote, "was no longer an abstraction, but a series of afflictions."

As industries crumbled and breadlines grew, some of the unemployed turned to revolutionary ideologies, while most embraced social democratic reforms. The political loyalties of the thirties, which shaped the war and the character of governments and economic policies long after it, suggest the broader political significance of unemployment. Orwell's "haunting" effectively transformed people's notions of society and government, but most of them wanted only security—the welfare state, not revolution. As this political legacy of unemployment begins to recede today, the problem itself—the periodic violence of the market and the resulting panic of unemployment —remain permanently etched in the minds of those who lived through it, just as it is surely inscribed in our future.

James R. Barrett

Individualism

A warning—to historians, to readers of this book. Whatever the appeal of photographs as unfiltered apertures to objective reality, they are less and more than that. The hand on the camera, it turns out, is quicker than the eye. Poet Archibald MacLeish, in his 1938 collection of photographs and free verse entitled *Land of the Free,* presented the picture on the left as an icon of American individualism: the freedom and fulfillment represented by Coke, car, and eyes cast toward the horizon; the individual, bolstered by stalwart rural values, as master of all he surveys, obligated only to his dreams. This photo, it seems, also captures the trajectory of the twentieth century, glorifying a world of free and equal opportunity as individualism supplants notions that "it takes a village" to define our identities and our boundaries.

But the picture on the right reminds us that a snapshot is just that: a partial representation, a product of a particular angle of vision, frozen in a moment of time. The Clark, Mississippi, plantation owner foregrounded in Dorothea Lange's full original 1936 photograph still appears as master of all he surveys, but now this mastery calls attention to the human relationships that sustain him. "Free," Lange urged viewers of her images to recognize, was not equal—certainly not to the extent that one person's freedom was purchased at the expense of the subjugation of another. Extending the frame field of the photograph on the left flips individualism into images of racism and subordination, juxtaposing the plantation owner's proud independence with the constricted prospects of what could well be his own sharecroppers on the stoop behind him.

It is inconceivable that this irony escaped MacLeish. The very title *Land of the Free* was a sardonic lament. MacLeish cropped the Lange photograph to create a nostalgic straw man, almost an optical allusion. He then deployed other pictures by Lange from the renowned Farm Security Administration's photographic indictment of American poverty and human misery to present a Depression-Era vista of eroded fields, eroded freedom, and eroded human beings. How fitting that such an arresting image of individualism could be plucked out of a photograph that spotlighted the inequality that MacLeish decried. It is an irony that persists today, particularly when following the example of Lange's photo by looking beyond comforting borders—of individual, of class, of nation.

Mark H. Leff

Fallingwater

No single residence has so often and so consistently been voted by professionals as the century's most influential American building (and no American architect's work so omnipresent among the voters) as Frank Lloyd Wright's 1937 Kaufmann House at Bear Run, Pennsylvania, called "Fallingwater."

Wright insisted that form, environment, and function be integrated into his organic designs, and he popularized techniques such as reinforced concrete that would change forever the way the world would use and think about living space. Wright's modernist Prairie School stripped us of the pretensions of nineteenth-century classical design and circumvented the European airs of Beaux Arts. When he reached the height of his influence in the mid-1930s, his vision of the planned community, Broadacre City, sought to reconcile fundamental trends in modern life that remain as pivotal issues in global culture seventy years later: how to negotiate between our increasingly centralized communications systems with their inevitable cultural homogenization and a living environment that places high value on ever-dispersing habitation patterns with our quest for separate identities.

Space and ornament that surround our daily lives have been profoundly altered during this century. Uncluttered, clean lines are a reflection of our society's fascination with functionalism merged with a quest for unencumbered, even undisciplined, freedom. Gone the exclusive, architect-designed dwelling; enter the mass-produced Sears house, or the mail-order blueprints from Wright himself in the 1907 *Ladies Home Journal.*

Home is more private than in times past, as we retreat from the dangers of physical contact and shared space with others. Gone the front porch with the decline of neighborhood street life; enter an ideal of a bathroom for every denizen in the land and alarm devices to warn off the unexpected visitor. Home is also more public, more open to diverse influences, from eclectic design to eccentric visitors. Gone the formal parlor, then the dining room, as the center for entertaining the select; enter the "rec room," the family room, now the deck with its built-in entertainment center for receiving anybody. Home is an extension of modern man and woman, stripped of top hats, formal attire, parasols, and hoops. Wright's open planning simply removed an en-vironment for excessive ornamentation, "gingerbread," inside and out. Enter the simple line, the cold, the bare, a "modern" style not meant to be too cozy and certainly not cluttered. Home is now largely ungendered, devoid of the private kitchen space once the domain of women, or the cellar workplace reserved for men. Gone the sewing room with the seamstress role, the parlor for after-dinner smokes; enter the megafreezer for frozen dinners.

Fallingwater symbolizes the very best and most enduring of modernist ideas on the creation of unencumbered, open space, of organic architecture, of living horizontally and eliminating the superfluous. Yet, there is something fundamental about clutter in human nature that also challenged the transfer of modernism into the home and eventually provoked a reaction against it. This may best be illustrated by Wright's most pedestrian invention, the basement-substitute known as the "carport," which did not endure, presumably because of the public display it gave to of our twentieth-century clutter.

Charles C. Stewart

World's Fair

In the course of the late 1930s thousands of workers transformed an old garbage dump in the New York borough of Queens into the 1939–40 New York World's Fair. For the price of a five-cent subway ride and a seventy-five-cent admission fee, some fifty-seven million attendees could sample personally "the wonders of contemporary life." The symbol of the fair was the trylon and the perisphere: the trylon was a slender three-sided pylon that—at 610 feet—was taller than the Washington monument; the perisphere—as tall as an eighteen-story building—was the largest globe ever built. Displayed on posters, postage stamps, magazine covers, advertisements, and souvenirs, the trylon and perisphere constituted the first major piece of abstract art to which many Americans had been exposed, but the rest of the New York World's Fair was anything but abstract.

Since the middle of the nineteenth century, industrial states had mounted periodic expositions to showcase the goods produced by their nationals and by others. Although London's Great Exhibition of 1851 had led the way, it was the French who were to produce such international displays of culture and machinery most frequently during the next half-century. American exposi-

tions tied the French example to the celebration of key historical anniversaries. The best-remembered example is the Chicago Exposition of 1893, which marked the four hundredth anniversary of Columbus's arrival—one year late. The New York World's fair of 1939 was inspired by the 150th anniversary of the inauguration of George Washington.

What took place at these showcases of modern architecture, national prestige, and international commercial competition? The 1893 Chicago fair boasted its entertainment "Midway" as well as scientific exhibits, and visitors to the New York fair in 1939 may well have been more impressed by the simulated 250-foot parachute jump than by the first speech by a president to be shown on television, or the first color film for home movie cameras, or the first look at nylon or through Plexiglas. General Motors sponsored a "Futurama" in which seated viewers moved on a track into the American landscape of the 1960s, a harmonious world of multilane express highways, radio-controlled cars, massive suspension bridges, high-rise buildings, and electrified farms.

The fair of 1939–40 could poignantly serve at once as a last act of an "age of innocence" in American life, as a declaration of closure on the ravages of the

Great Depression, and as a defiant assertion of neutrality in a world becoming polarized by conflict in Europe and East Asia. By the time the fair closed many of the sixty nations who were exhibitors were caught up in World War II; and the pavilion representing Czechoslovakia had been made redundant by Hitler even before the fair opened its doors.

The idea of such international expositions remained viable despite hot war and cold war, and during the years after 1945 there were to be successful fairs in cities as varied as Brussels and Seattle, New York and Montreal. Since the 1970s, however, this prototypical late nineteenth- and early twentieth-century phenomenon of temporary multinational "cities" and showcases has begun to die out. International economic competition continues, and our global economy may be more interdependent than ever, but in an age of readily accessible jet travel and of televised and computerized "virtual reality," temporary world fairs may have become both too costly and not real enough. An analogous form of peaceful competition among nations but one more suited to the media needs of the last quarter of the century, the Olympic Games, continues to thrive.

Walter L. Arnstein

Olympics

Individual achievement and national glory, international cooperation and nationalist rivalry, athletics and politics, gender and race, the West and the Rest. The Olympic Games provide an excellent lens to capture the dynamics and aspirations of the twentieth century.

Originally scheduled to commence in 1900 to coincide with the beginning of the new century, the first modern Olympic games in fact were held in 1896 in Athens, four years later in Paris, and thereafter at four-year intervals in the great capitals of the world. The selection of the sites was largely the work of the principal organizer of the modern Olympics, a young French nobleman, Baron Pierre de Coubertin (1863–1937), who was driven by two contradictory impulses: a sense that athletic competition was a universal feature of human history best captured in the ancient games at Mt. Olympus and a belief that national strength rested on the moral and physical condition of the citizenry. For the rest of the century, the Games would feature both individual athletes and national teams.

Just as the Olympic Games themselves embodied contradictions between individual and archaic aspirations and nationalist rivalries, accounts of the significant moments in the history of the Games reflect the national filters through which they are constructed. American histories of the Olympic Games often emphasize the achievements of individual minority athletes (hoping to reinforce American national values of individualist pluralism): Jim Thorpe, Jesse Owens, Patricia McCormick—each name embodies certain American attitudes about national identity.

The 1936 Berlin Games represented another national approach to the Olympics. Hosting the Games became a symbol of desperately wanted international recognition and frantic national display. For the Nazis, 1936 was a grand coming out, in which the jagged arms of the swastika repeatedly hooked themselves into the Five Rings of the Olympic movement, the one symbol lending credence to the other. In the photograph itself, the excitement of the American team's arrival at the Berlin train station is overwhelmed by a sense of peril (look at the anxious faces) at the sight of the heavy-handed political salutes. In a flash, the expectations of the athlete had collided uneasily with the purposes of the state.

The history of the Olympics in the latter half of the twentieth century is closely tied with the politics of decolonization and greater attempts to accommodate the non-West. Following the 1936 Berlin Games, the 1964 Tokyo Olympics anchored a new postwar use of the games to signify national rehabilitation and legitimacy. Following Japan's successful model, many nations —especially outside the West, found in the Olympics not merely the story of individual athletic victory but the possibility of national redemption. For South Korea, the 1988 Summer Games in Seoul was a monumental national celebration; while for China its failure to win the hosting of the 2000 Olympics was a crushing defeat; and for Israel (and Germany), the 1972 Munich massacre represented unrelieved national tragedy.

Born with the twentieth century, the Olympic Games are intertwined with its history: the century's happy celebration of individual excellence, its stubborn insistence on competition, its right-minded avowal of concord and toleration, its unending fascination with nationalist display.

Kevin M. Doak

Chaplin

In his anti-Nazi film, *The Great Dictator,* Charles Chaplin challenged the Hollywood conventions of his day. In contrast to the other studios, which until Pearl Harbor scrupulously avoided making anti-Nazi films—either for fear of offending pro-German sentiment or of losing revenues by mixing politics and entertainment—Chaplin released *The Great Dictator* in October 1940. As one who pioneered in so many aspects of the film industry, he was willing to take the risk. His life reflects the conflict between those who would use the new mass media of the twentieth century for serious art and social commentary and those who would confine it to consumerism and entertainment.

In *The Great Dictator* Chaplin used the strongest weapon in his arsenal, ridicule, to fight Hitler. He played both the dictator, Adenoid Hynkel, a caricature of Hitler, and his exact double, a little Jewish barber, drawing on his previous "tramp" character from silent film days. Using mock German, Chaplin ridiculed Hitler's bombastic speeches; he parodied the goose step and made fun of an absurd Mussolini character. In the film's most memorable scene Hynkel, in a fit of megalomania, gracefully bounces the world in the form of a balloon off his hands, arms and feet. The film concludes when the Jewish barber, in a case of mistaken identity, impersonates Hynkel and before a vast audience makes an idealistic speech denouncing nationalism, war, armaments, and race hatred.

Unfortunately, events in Europe had moved too fast for the film. When the movie was conceived in 1938, Hitler was a boasting bully ripe for satirical treatment. By October 1940 he had conquered most of Europe and was a serious threat to the entire world. Still, the public was ready to see Hitler ridiculed, and the film was well received, especially in war-torn Britain, Chaplin's childhood home, where he was still a citizen and a public idol.

Because of his outspoken sympathy for the Soviet allies during the war and his defiance of popular conventions, Chaplin was harassed in the United States by the FBI and in 1952 he was exiled from that country. His last films were boycotted by frightened Hollywood distributors. It was only in 1972 that the Hollywood magnates felt it was now safe to invite him back to America and to acknowledge his major contributions to the development of an industry that he had so enriched.

Blair B. Kling

Women's War

When the classic work on the history of women comes to be written, the biggest force for change in their lives will turn out to have been war." So wrote Max Lerner in World War II, just as *Life* printed this impossibly Freudian photo of women aircraft workers polishing bomber nose cones. Lerner had a point. With the partial and notable exception of Nazi Germany, where the sanctification of Aryan motherhood and the exploitation of foreign captive labor worked to confine most women to "Kinder, Küche, Kirche" in the face of desperate production needs, twentieth-century wars have propelled women into new roles: ambulance drivers and voters in World War I and its aftermath; and in World War II resistance fighters in Europe, conscripted war workers in Britain, and combat soldiers and most of the industrial workforce in the Soviet Union. In the United States, where the female paid work-force rocketed by 50 percent and the number of factory jobs held by women doubled (although still only one in four wives worked outside the home, most of them in predominantly female job settings), "Rosie the Riveter" became a symbol of home front dedication to the war.

Yet this photographic image proved peculiarly appropriate. Government propaganda urged women into war jobs not as an opportunity for emancipation, and often not even as a patriotic exercise in commitment to the national cause, but because "by working on a war job . . . a woman is protecting her own loved ones from death on the battlefield." War work, in other words, could be cast as an affirmation of women's family obligations rather than as a departure from them. The war's prime cultural heroes, after all, were male "warriors"—soldiers who tended to picture themselves as fighting to protect an "American Way of Life" that included a traditional, woman-centered hearth, home, and family. It proved to be a short step from nose cone polishers to a cult of domesticity in which bras themselves resembled nose cones.

At war's end, the call for Rosies to serve their men again, this time by yielding their jobs for returning soldiers, lent a gendered meaning to the term "pink slip," and social supports for working women, such as federally financed child care centers, vanished. Even during the war itself, the American "baby boom" had begun with earlier marriages and higher birthrates. Other forces soon brought more women, particularly wives without young children to care for, into the paid labor force. But the jobs themselves were more "traditional" ones (many Rosies could not even receive un-employment benefits if they insisted on seeking riveting jobs rather than office work). It would take more than a war to banish traditional definitions of femininity. At century's end, Rosie the Riveter was still doing battle.

Mark H. Leff

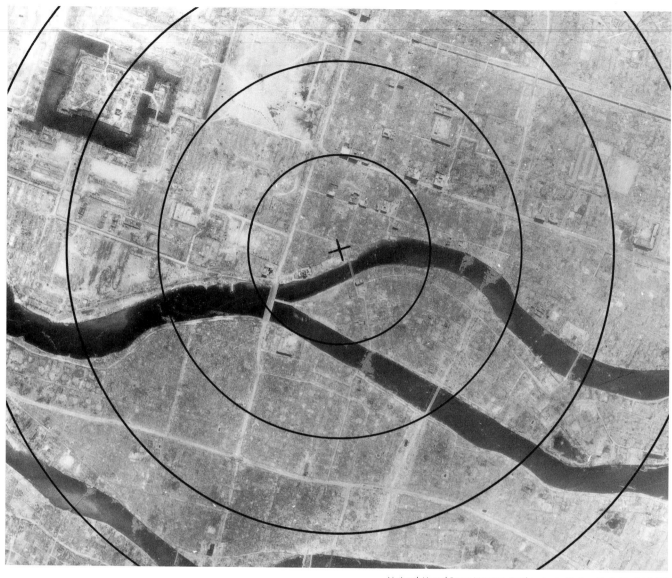

Mass Death

On 6 August 1945, humanity crossed a threshold to enter a new, dangerous age from which there will never be a retreat. On that day, a single bomb wiped out an entire city, Hiroshima. Reconnaissance photographs of the city immediately before and after the blast reveal how this awful child of modern science leveled a forest of buildings, killed over one hundred thousand people in a split second, and left a desert of mute destruction. Although other Allied bombing raids had been nearly as destructive in Hamburg, Dresden, and Tokyo, Hiroshima was different because its obliteration was instantaneous, revealing at once the catastrophic potential of the nuclear age.

By making the destruction of hu-

manity so literal, war had become absolute. Nuclear warfare's complete compass had finally exposed the basically nihilist core to state-on-state conflicts which the great Prussian theorist Clausewitz had only imagined. Yet paradox abounded on this extreme. In his 1915 novel, *The World Set Free,* H. G. Wells foretold weapons so terrible that they made warfare impossible, and his vision was embraced by scientists who first proposed the Manhattan Project. Thus far, nuclear and thermonuclear weapons have conformed to Wells's fiction because they have forestalled all-out conflict among members of the so-called nuclear club. In the cold war, the great powers adopted policies such as massive retaliation, or mutually assured destruction, suitably known as MAD; and suicide thereby became a reasonable form of self-defense—an ultimate paradox.

John A. Lynn

The Holocaust

In 1989, witnesses stood amidst the rubble of the Berlin Wall and wondered whether the twentieth century was beginning to heal itself. The collapse of the Soviet Union and the wave of free elections around the world nourished the hope that a peculiarly demented, if modern, itinerary had come to an end. Nazism and Communism, those stern tyrannies of war and revolution, no longer appeared formidable foes. It makes some sense to consider the years 1914 and 1989 as beginning and end points to a particularly violent passage that has now been successfully crossed.

Yet at the center of the century a stillness continues to unsettle the navigator. The Holocaust, the destruction of European Jews at the hands of the Nazis, is at once an outrage that seems explicable in terms of National Socialism and anti-Semitism and also a trauma that silences explanation. The Holocaust resists easy formulations about twentieth-century history because it pulls at notions of what can be explained and translated and understood.

The victims of the crime cannot speak because the vast majority of European Jews whom the Nazis transported to the edges of forests and the gas chambers in death camps were killed. What happened in the death camps remains a solitary experience that cannot be well translated or poignantly represented. For their part, the German killers endeavored to wipe away the traces of their crimes and to keep their intentions hidden from the victims themselves.

As a result, the Holocaust is often thought to be an extremely strange and complex bureaucratic process in which victims quickly disappeared and in which perpetrators had little comprehensive knowledge and accordingly shared little responsibility. What has not been remembered and what has been willfully forgotten shapes much of our knowledge of the Holocaust.

Because of the difficulty of speaking for others, historians have always had trouble making definitive sense out of the Holocaust and artists are pushed to the very limits of representation. As a result, the dark center of the century is perhaps best understood in terms of these difficulties, as a trauma that has disrupted the ways and means of telling about what has happened, a trauma that must be approached by constantly listening to the testimony of victims and perpetrators, again and again. The Holocaust has unsteadied the very process of accounting for crimes and of explaining history. A few artifacts remain, however.

This photograph depicts German Wehrmacht soldiers browsing through the snapshots they have taken of a shooting of Jewish civilians. The entire sequence, which ends with the inspection of the images, captures soldiers rounding up Serbian Jews sometime in 1942, marching them into the forest, forcing them to dig their graves, and then murdering them. The photographs not only show the soldiers killing but narrating the killing in which they have just played active roles and in which they have found some meaning and evident satisfaction.

The inset image is one of the personal photographs Jewish victims carried with them before they were killed at Majdanek.

Peter Fritzsche

Central State Archive of Film, Photo and Phonographic Documents, Russia, courtesy of USHMM Photo Archives

Etablissement Cinématographique et Photographique des Armées, Paris, courtesy of USHMM Photo Archives

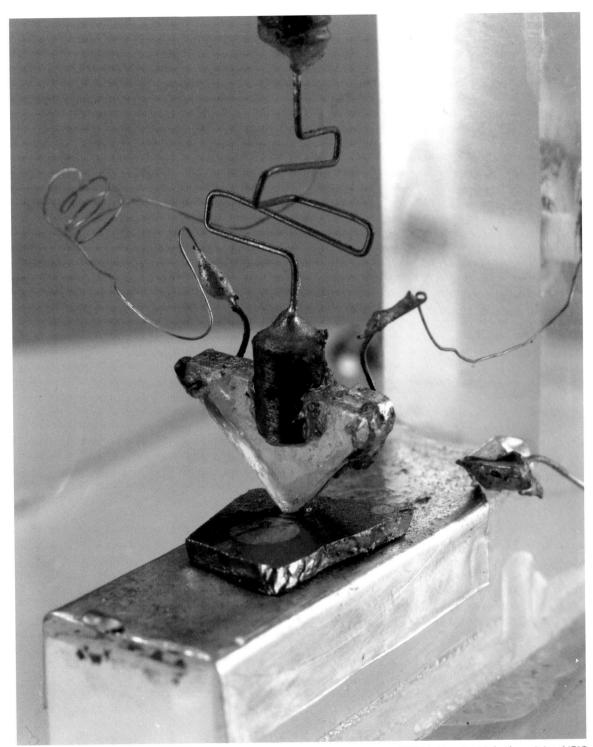

Transistor

April 4, 1968. I arrived in the Saharan camp in the late afternoon after five hours of bone-rattling travel across dunes, five hours without catching sight of more than a few head of camels on a landscape of sand and scrub. A tent was hastily pitched in our honor, large enough to seat twenty on the rich Moroccan carpets spread across the sand floor. Local rites of hospitality began: a heavily-sugared mint tea common to Muslim societies stretching eastward to China was served. After evening prayers, conversation was muffled, respectful of the awe-inspiring drama of crimson sky at day's end, the infinity of the Saharan landscape at dusk. At once, "Why are they burning Detroit?" came the question from my host. Minutes before our arrival word had come by transistor from Cairo and Paris, Moscow and Washington of urban eruptions across America in the wake of the assassination of Martin Luther King.

The point-contact transistor, invented at the Bell labs in 1947 by Illinois physicists John Bardeen and Walter Brattain, revolutionized electronic sound communication at mid-century. This was the mid-century equivalent to the invention of the triode in 1906 for amplifying current, which had led to the development of numerous sophisticated types of vacuum tubes, devices that gave birth to the radio as an ever-increasing mainstay of national communication in the first half of the century. After 1947 the transistor, paired with the AA battery, was to have the same effect, but now globally, even into my Saharan tent. Within just twenty years, the transistor democratized access to large and diverse quantities of information that had formerly been the preserve of relatively few, urbanized, electrified islands on the globe.

The arrival of the transistor on the very eve of the explosion of the colonial empires may well have been the miniature fuse that ignited mass political consciousness for populations from India to the Sahara desert. It certainly brought down state borders that had once served to control information flows and created whole new arenas for exerting and contesting state influence. Superpowers vied for the attention of millions of global listeners and constructed new ways to invent or at least to reshape the present as well as the past. Global literacy rapidly emerged as an aural phenomenon. The owner of a transistor (the word "radio" quickly became redundant) was empowered and co-opted into the networks of invisible electronic threads tightening and shrinking, creating and homogenizing a global culture.

Forty years after its creation the vacuum tube begot the transistor, twenty years later the transistor begot the integrated circuit. We close the century with predictions that computer memories will double annually for the next forty years. The resulting velocity and volume of information outstrips our ability to understand what we know. But the fact remains that even my Saharan tents will remain forever pitched next door to Detroit.

Charles C. Stewart

Migrants

An Italian family arrives at Ellis Island in 1905, Mexican workers wade the Rio Grande in 1948, and an Indian worker fleeing war-torn Kuwait in 1991 shows his papers; "boat people" become a modern metaphor for the dispossessed, the landless. Although we tend to think of our world in terms of distinct nations with precise boundaries, these pictures are a reminder that for millions of people the land under their feet may not be their own. Migration is one of the reasons why boundaries are in fact permeable and national cultures are malleable. Humanity has always been on the move, but twice in this century—at its beginning and toward its end—international migration has reached epic proportions. The greatest age of world migration so far was between 1840 and 1940: the movement peaked just before World War I, with immigration to the United States surpassing a million in some years. The end of the century has brought another surge of world migration, and again the United States is part of this trend, with its annual intake of immigrants close to pre–World War I levels.

Why? Who are these people? About a fifth of international migrants today are refugees, but the vast majority are laborers going where the money is. Since the creation of a world economy five hundred years ago, most migration has been labor migration, and the labor (including enslaved labor) has gone where growing economies created demand. Beyond that, modern migration patterns reflect other kinds of linkages between countries and regions—investment, trade, and the various other economic, cultural, and political ties left in the wake of colonialism. Networks formed by earlier generations of migrants and returnees make it possible for someone to imagine making a living in a distant land, and once there to find housing and work. Migration networks often channel people to specific countries, industries, and "ethnic" neighborhoods: Yemenis to the auto industry in Dearborn, Michigan, for example, or Filipina domestics to Hong Kong.

A century ago the majority of emigrants worldwide were Europeans destined for other European countries and the Americas, Asiatic Russia, Australia, New Zealand, and a handful of African colonies. Additionally, tens of millions of Indians, Chinese, and Japanese contract laborers were recruited to work in the colonial possessions of Africa and Asia, as well as in the Americas. The pattern of world migration since World War II reflects the changing world economy and its increasing globalization. Europe, long accustomed to intracontinental migration, received millions of migrants from Asia, Africa, and the Caribbean during the 1950s and 1960s. In the 1970s the Middle Eastern oil-producing countries began importing workers from south and East Asia, partly reducing their traditional reliance on Arab migrant labor. More recently, the industrializing countries of East Asia have made use of migrant workers from their less developed neighbors. North America has become a magnet for Latin Americans and Asians.

The fact that migration is economically necessary does not mean the migrants are always welcome. Countries newly experiencing immigration, such

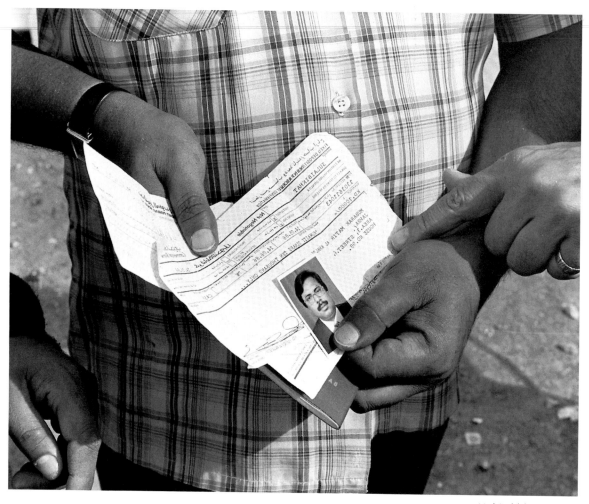

as the Arab oil countries and Japan, do not consider allowing permanent residence to their "guest workers," much less citizenship. Germany and France have large resident Turkish and North African communities which maintain elements of their cultural and national identities, challenging traditional notions of what it means to become German or French. Comparatively less cultural assimilation is expected of newcomers to the United States, but the current wave of immigration has still produced a backlash. Are these tensions due to rigid ideas about what constitutes civic society? Are they about racism? Or are they a part of a more profound contradiction that has taken shape in the twentieth century? In an era in which most people think of the world in terms of distinct nations, an ever-mounting movement of capital, goods, and—especially—migrants defies traditional political frontiers and challenges the boundaries of our own identities.

Kenneth M. Cuno

Evita Perón

"Hello Buenos Aires!
Get this—just look at me, dressed up
  somewhere to go
We'll put on a show!
Take me in at your flood, give me
  speed, give me lights,
  set me humming
Shoot me up with your blood, wine
  me up with your nights,
  watch me coming
All I want is a whole lot of excess
Tell the singer this is where I am
  playing

Stand back Buenos Aires!
Because you ought to know what'cha
  gonna get in me
Just a little touch of star quality!"

—From the musical *Evita*, 1976,
lyrics by Tim Rice

Eva Maria Duarte de Perón (1919–52)
became a legend in her own time. She
demonstrated to the world what a poor
girl of illegitimate birth from one of
those shabby country towns of the
Argentine pampas could accomplish.
And the world was impressed, wining
and dining her at elaborate state dinners with European heads of state,
charming her at a tête-a-tête with Aris-
totle Onassis in Monte Carlo's Hotel de
Paris, and broadcasting her glamorous
image as her country's first lady in
glitzy photo spreads in *Life Magazine*.
She was a Latin American version of
Jacqueline Kennedy a full decade in
advance.

The power of legend arises out of

faith in half-truths and broad popular
belief in life stories that vastly tran-
scend the ordinary. Modern legends
draw their power from crystallizing the
hopes and fears of communities. Evita
encapsulated the longing of many common women to escape the drudgery
and oppression of domestic life. But
Evita's life was a cautionary tale: her
own empowerment became a central
storyline of the construction of a harsh,
patriarchal populist and authoritarian
regime. Her climb to the heights of
fame and fortune would be cast in the
images of diverse traditional roles of
women. Was this a story of the tremendous expansion of women's roles in
modern society? Or was it a glorifica-
tion of subservient, male-dominated
women?

Evita was everything to Argentina:
whore, seductress, wily politician,
power grabber and manipulator, bene-
factress, mother of the nation, saint.
Coming to Buenos Aires at seventeen,
during the mid-1930s, she launched a
successful career as an actress in theaters, movies, and especially radio
dramas, a rapidly expanding world
of commercial popular entertainment
where life was hard and loose and most
women had a leading man. At age
twenty-five she became mistress and
one year later the wife of Colonel Juan
Domingo Perón, one of the most powerful figures of the military regime in
power. From that moment on her fame
spiraled upward, powered by the best
acting roles to be had and her growing
prominence in the nationalist populist

World Wide Photo

Courtesy, Archivo General de la Nación, Argentina

political campaign of Perón himself.

Evita forged strong clientelistic bonds with the *descamisados,* the millions of new industrial workers who became the social backbone of the Peronist regime between 1946 and 1955. Extravagantly dressed and bejeweled, she dispensed favors to the poor who were lining up at her own charitable foundation for material help. She would kiss babies and hug the sick and weary, "dispensing Christian love." She delivered rousing demagogic speeches at party congresses and demonstrations. She used her influence to cut down anybody endangering her husband's power and stature. The authoritarian Peronist machinery of state made her an icon of the nation, quietly removing material from her acting days from public access and distributing a mature motherly image of the less-than-thirty-year-old first lady everywhere, on stamps, in offices, and in the streets. Yet all this served the aggrandizement of a hierarchical, male-dominated authoritarian regime, whose font of power was her husband. When she died of cancer, at the height of her power in 1952, she was made a martyr for the Peronist cause, and the Buenos Aires newspaper vendors union proposed her for canonization to the Vatican.

Evita's meteoric rise encapsulated many of the paradoxes of women's roles in the most developed countries of the world during the mid-twentieth century. The divas of Hollywood, from Greta Garbo to Marilyn Monroe, were prototypes of the adored but highly fragile woman: glamorous, sensuous, successful beyond comparison in the world of make-believe, yet also vulnerable, in need of a strong man. By the 1930s and 1940s a generation of young women enjoyed new areas of economic freedom in modest white-collar positions, before retiring to the harbor of matrimony and homemaking.

Evita became a legend for Latin America and beyond because her public life symbolized new aspirations and stark limitations in the lives of many women coming of age between the 1930s and 1950s. Women were mobilized for empowering virile nations and efficient industrial economies, whose male leadership was doubted by few. And now, as the century draws to an end, Hollywood mobilizes another ambiguous icon of femininity, Madonna, to universalize the commercial promise of the legend of Evita Perón.

Nils P. Jacobsen

Barbie

This is THE doll of the late twentieth century. The creation of Barbie in 1959 transformed the idea of a girl's doll. In the days B.B., as in "Before Barbie," dolls for children were baby dolls, intended to train girls into their future role as mothers.

Barbie, however, was a full-figured adult female. If the baby doll signified a girl's future as mother; Barbie signaled a new future for girls as sex object. Probably Barbie's most notable feature were her breasts: large and pointed, the preferred shape of the 1950s. Her feet also took an unnatural shape. Instead of a baby doll's curled toes or flat feet, Barbie's were shaped to fit the spike heels that fashionable women of the West wore in the 1950s. She was an anatomical wonder: even when she went barefoot, she walked on her toes. She first appeared with a blonde pony-tail, in a black and white striped bathing suit of the sort worn by beauty contestants. Barbie's purpose in life was to be sexy and to collect a large wardrobe. These were to become Barbie's most controversial, and perhaps most admired, features. Barbie is now beloved by millions and universally known, but perhaps oddly, not a doll that snuggles in bed as easily as did some of her predecessors.

Barbie has been criticized as a toy that represented society's worst attitudes toward women: she seemed to embody the idea that women were sex objects, whose purpose was to please men. Barbie's very shape, many argue, taught girls to aspire to a standard of beauty impossible to achieve, thus contributing to self-hatred among women, as well as to anorexia.

Recently, young feminists who played with Barbie and see her as fun, not simply evil, have resuscitated Barbie's reputation. These adults remember that Barbie had other meanings when they were children. Barbie served as sex object for kids to play out their own budding interests in the kinds of relationships now imagined between Barbie and Ken, or Barbie and Midge. (It is likely that Ken and GI Joe fooled around together too.)

Barbie has proved responsive to her critics and to her times. As she approaches forty, her huge wardrobe now includes accessories to maintain her health and her figure through exercise: surfboards, bicycles, and tennis racquets, all in pink. The athletic Barbie's body has accommodated this new activity: she now has flat feet. Barbie has also gone professional: she has outfits that indicate possible futures as

a physician or an astronaut, in addition to her standard fashion model mode. And Barbie has gone multicultural; there are now African American Barbies with dark skin and black hair (very long, no afros yet) and Japanese Barbies. But her features have not changed despite changes in skin color and ethnicity, and she has never been made a mother. Children, the researchers tell us, still prefer the blond Barbie.

What of Barbie's future in the twenty-first century when she turns fifty or sixty? Perhaps she will be joined by an equally popular adult male doll for boys who doesn't need to wear camouflage and who can be her equal in the adoring eyes of boys as well as girls. She will surely remain a symbol of the American obsession with the breast and the blonde. In this photo an East German child embraces both a new Barbie and American consumerism. It is clear that children (and adults) find meaning in Barbie in many ways; her resilience, her adaptability, her very plasticity in changing times may best assure her a place in the iconography of the twenty-first century.

Leslie J. Reagan

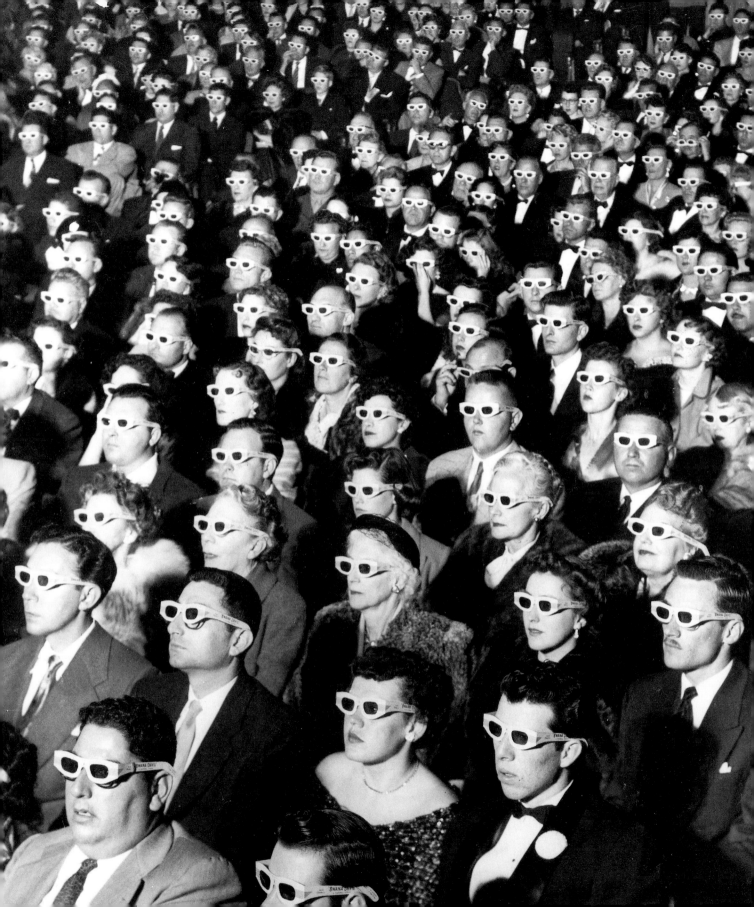

Movie Audience

Masked in order to see the world anew, the movie audience enacts a century of hopes and fears. By 1900, an already extensive commerce in popular culture exploded in technological wonder. This was best seen in the picture palace, where motion wrote in lightening strokes about democratized art and collective dreams. For popular audiences and social prophets alike, the palace heralded a new utopia where leisure, not work, would provide self-definition, fulfillment, even enlightenment for the masses. Here the vitality of the folk and the gravity of the erudite might mingle, making culture fun and accessible for everyone.

But this promised land remained remote, especially in the eyes of the prophets. The shining realm of freedom fell under the shadow of big business and big government; the folk seemed too eager to trade their quaint traditions for prefabricated kitsch. Regional vernaculars, family traditions, and democratic ideals seemed to get lost, claimed by Sony or Disney as marketable nostalgia. It is this kind of nightmare that is evoked by the photograph of the movie audience in their eerily acquiescent three-dimensional glasses. By mid-century, critics were using this image to depict mass culture as a mental cage—a "society of the spectacle" where the technologies of pleasure and creativity delivered only vulgarity and conformity.

But the audiences themselves might tell a different, more complicated story. The popular arts did transform old loyalties and inherited traditions, but they also appealed to new sensitivities and generated new communities at the picture palace and its outposts—the record player, radio, the magazine. If this wasn't a promised land, it might point there. American audiences demonstrated this optimism when they forged consumer hopes into industrial demands; overseas, audiences imagined the Good Life as the America they saw at the movies. Meanwhile, the seemingly lockstepping spectators were as silly as they were somber. They took their glasses off and wandered on to other entertainments like the television set and computer monitor, which reshaped the relations between the remote and the intimate. The promised land of leisure thereby took on ever-changing dimensions of freedom and discipline, whimsy and anxiety.

Kathryn J. Oberdeck

Keystone-Mast Collection, UCR/California Museum of Photography, Neg.# (ACT)8627

Icons of Empire

A zeppelin, symbol of German imperial pretensions and European might that was to demonstrate Germany's credentials as she entered the twentieth century on near-equal footing with the other great European empires in Africa, the Middle East, and Asia. Egypt, strategic hinge of British imperial possessions in India and Africa at the opening of the century and site of the Suez Canal that linked Queen Victoria's "Jewel in the Crown" of the Empire with the motherland. Pyramids at Giza, monuments to a much earlier royal hegemony, icons of authority that remind us of the antiquity of such public display of political symbols. Arab travelers, pausing to take in the ancient icons juxtaposed against the recently rekindled pan-Arab world of their own for which no public icon was possible under British occupation, and the rival German airship hovering at a distance. In this one photograph only the look on the face of the observers is hidden from our survey of four layers of political iconography which, in many respects, came into its own as a twentieth-century by-product of the nation-state.

In few sites was this better demonstrated than the cities of the old British Empire where statues of Queen Victoria, public spaces named in her honor, and portraits of her presence decorated territory covering one-fifth of the earth's surface. The statue pictured here is stored in an enclosure behind the Bombay Zoo. Queen Victoria, proclaimed empress of India in 1876, was meant to be a mother figure for the masses and a titular head for the native princes, much taken themselves with the regal pomp and ceremony her symbolic presence incited. In an old lithograph described by Paul Scott in one of his novels, Queen Victoria is depicted on her throne surrounded by children representing all the races of the empire wearing their native costumes and seated happily at the feet or on the lap of the motherly queen. The lithograph embodies sentiments that were unlikely to have been held by many of her subjects, but it does confirm the identity of a motherly icon, now only an immovable and decaying lump of concrete relegated to storage dumps across the former empire.

Victoria, like the skeleton of the zeppelin and the many versions of the Arc de Triomphe in the one-time colonies where French is still spoken, has joined the graveyards of imperial monuments, but she remains testimony to the importance of these icons to political overrule and cultural domination. Where they are too massive to be removed, their next life has frequently been as a museum piece, as an exposé of former grandeur, an anti-icon to contrast with the rational use of power today. The history of the twentieth century could be written in these public displays of authority, or rather in the discarded and disintegrating icons, monuments to human optimism, to racism, to the significance of the nation-state as living actor in our lives, and to something very basic in the human condition that finds comfort in heroes and heroic symbols.

Blair B. Kling

Blair Kling

83

[Frontispiece]   THE AUTHOR   [Photo by Brian Cobbold]

FACING MOUNT KENYA

The Tribal Life of the Gikuyu

by

JOMO KENYATTA

with an Introduction by

B. MALINOWSKI

Ph.D. (Cracow); D.Sc. (London); Hon. D.Sc. (Harvard)

Professor of Anthropology in the University of London

SECKER AND WARBURG

1953

Kenyatta

The photograph is a simple one: a young African man wearing ancestral dress thoughtfully fondles a spear. It appeared in 1937 as a frontispiece to *Facing Mount Kenya* and is a portrait of the book's author, Jomo Kenyatta. But there is nothing simple either about the photograph or about its subject.

Jomo Kenyatta was born sometime in the early 1890s as Kamau Ngengi. He was baptized in 1914 as Johnstone Kamau. In the 1920s he worked in Nairobi, where he owned a motorbike and was known as Johnstone Kamau. In 1929 he left for England, where he settled and studied anthropology at the London School of Economics under Professor Bronisław Malinowski. In 1937 he published *Facing Mount Kenya*. By then he had become Jomo Kenyatta. In presenting himself to his readers, Kenyatta forswore European clothes in favor of those worn by his Gikuyu ancestors, clothes which he had worn in none of his earlier photographs.

Facing Mount Kenya is a classic monograph, but it is far from a disinterested academic essay. Kenyatta was a political leader and the book reflects its author's concerns. Kenyatta had originally gone to London as a political representative, and, when he returned to Kenya in 1947, he immersed himself in anticolonial politics. In 1953, he was convicted of seditious activities. Ten years later he led Kenya to independence and became the president of his country until his death in 1977.

The photograph portrays Kenya's George Washington, father of his nation. But the photograph also speaks to the contradictory aspects of Kenyatta's political struggle, for which he had gone to prison and which he shared with a host of other twentieth-century leaders in Asia, Africa, and the Middle East. The book, *Facing Mount Kenya*, and its frontispiece photograph were artifacts of an industrial society which had been able to use systems of mass communication to subordinate colonial peoples. Yet Kenyatta used these artifacts to make claims for his people and for their different ways of making a livelihood and interpreting the world.

Facing Mount Kenya was, in fact, an early attempt to overthrow the relationship which linked the discipline of anthropology with colonial rule. British and French rulers turned to anthropologists and ethnologists in order to fashion more efficient, less abrasive techniques of domination. Many of the early classics of anthropology were produced by men employed by colonial governments. In *Facing Mount Kenya*, by contrast, Kenyatta, who is the subject of both colonialism and scientific inquiry, claimed to speak for himself and his own people. At the same time, he tried to strengthen Gikuyu identity by expressing it in a new form. The book challenged colonial terms of power.

Kamau Ngengi, Johnstone Kamau, Jomo Kenyatta—*Facing Mount Kenya* reflects the immense pressures which colonialism imposed on its subjects. Kenyatta embodied these pressures. They are the legacy of the peoples of Africa, Asia, and Latin America, whose countries were shaped by the imperial dominance of Western Europe and the United States. Raw materials for a global culture.

Donald E. Crummey

Cold War

Post–World War II baby boomers, we grew up under the constant threat of imminent nuclear annihilation. After our phonics lessons in school we learned the acronymic vocabulary of the nuclear age: DEW line, NATO, SAC, ICBM, CONLRAD. We watched instructional films and practiced our air-raid defense drills in the halls. Our parents stockpiled food and drinking water, as instructed by the Civil Defense Administration and by popular magazines, and they agonized over the moral dilemma of sharing their shelters: "when" the bomb came, would they let the neighbors in? Children took a perverse pride in boasting how important their neighborhoods were as Soviet targets: if your baseball team could not win the World Series, the next best thing was to live near a missile site or railway switching yard that was sure to be targeted.

The cold war's dark theme of impending annihilation usually remained background noise, except for moments of special tension, such as the Berlin crisis and airlift in 1948, the invasion of South Korea by the North. The H-bomb tests, which were televised, reminded us of our awesome fate as children of a superpower. During the Cuban missile crisis in 1962 we dusted off the canned goods and refilled water supplies in our basement shelters. By then we knew better than to think we could survive such an attack; Nevil Shute's *On the Beach* provided a compelling scenario for how the world might end. There were also moments of relaxation: the "spirit of Geneva" of 1955 followed the first summit talks between Soviet and U.S. leaders since Stalin met Truman in 1945, giving hope that the arms race could be managed.

Staatsbibliothek Preussischer Kulturbesitz, Berlin

Other test ban and arms limitations treaties followed, producing new acronyms—SALT, START—for schoolchildren to memorize. Tension and detente were the two seasons of the nuclear age.

Some of us assumed the enemy—the Soviet Union—was as implacably hostile to all our values as the most rabid anticommunists assured us they were. A few like me wondered, though, whether the truth about that society was not more complicated. I eventually made the serious scholarly study of the Soviet Union a lifetime project.

Even back in the 1950s, staring at my locker, trying to imagine the fireballs and shock waves we were training to endure, I wondered what might be going on in Soviet schools. Our missiles were pointed at them: what did they think about the prospect of immediate annihilation? Perhaps they were training in their classrooms, practicing civil defense, fitting on gas masks, learning to "drop, duck, and roll" under their desks. Weren't *we* just as ominous an enemy for them as they were for us? As it turns out, Soviet leaders were publicly silent about the ring of mis-

siles surrounding their country, even as they secretly devoted massive resources to the development of rival weapons. Were communal fallout shelters also in their five-year plans? We still do not know where the Soviet people fit into the equation of war, peace, and self-preservation. What did atomic culture Soviet-style look like? Probably they were just like us: alternating between the seasons of fear and relaxation and trying to get on with their lives.

Diane P. Koenker

Staatsbibliothek Preussischer Kulturbesitz, Berlin

Atomic Age

Apocalyptic terror and utopian fantasy were twinned responses to the technological futures that the century envisioned. Henry Adams, America's cranky "conservative Christian Anarchist," provided a classic expression of this ambivalent outlook as he surveyed the Paris Exposition of 1900. What was so captivating there, Adams insisted, was the display of new force. The motors stood for "the automobile, which . . . had become a nightmare at a hundred kilometers an hour, almost as destructive as the electric tram . . . and threatening to become as terrible as the locomotive." But if the machine was a dreadful truth, it also inspired reverent awe. "As he grew accustomed to the great gallery of machines," Adams continued, "he began to feel the forty-foot dynamos as a moral force, much as the early Christians felt the Cross. The planet itself seemed less impressive, in its old-fashioned, deliberate, annual or daily revolution, than this huge wheel, revolving within arm's-length and some vertiginous speed, and barely murmuring—scarcely humming an audible warning to stand a hair's breadth further for respect of power."

This emotional combination persisted in public reactions to the advent of the "Atomic Age" in 1945. The atom bomb's harvest of death and destruction confirmed Adams's most pessimistic prophecies (for him technological advance portended explosions that would "double in force and number every ten years"). But Ameri-

Staatsbibliothek Preussischer Kulturbesitz, Berlin

can observers discerned extravagant possibilities in what they heralded as a new historical epoch. Even the horrors of Hiroshima and Nagasaki affirmed a wonderful future for Atomic Age prophets, who believed such destruction would shock the globe into peace and common purpose.

The prophets also promised fantastic transformations for daily life in the new epoch. There were countless units of measure—a human fist, a railroad ticket, a puff of cigarette smoke, or, most popularly, a pea—for the astonishingly tiny amount of material that would be required to power Atomic Age industries and cities. Magazine writers forecast atomic cars, airplanes, and homes. At their most roseate, images of the Atomic Age promised a nuclear fix for the blights associated with technological improvements of the

past. Clogged, stifling industrial cities would disperse into the countryside, their inhabitants scattered across a newly pastoralized landscape. The conquest of nature that had been achieved by splitting the atom would finally heal modernity's alienation from nature.

Such fantasies paled before the frightening events at Three Mile Island and Chernobyl, and the struggle over where to dump the toxic waste of the brave new world. It has become clear that atomic power did not undo the paradoxes of technology or solve the global conflicts of human society. At the end of the century as at the beginning, machine dreams compete with the more sober reflections of those who try to redirect our awe to the planet's "old-fashioned, deliberate" methods.

Kathryn J. Oberdeck

Decolonization

When the familiar red, blue, and white crosshatched Union Jack was lowered in the new Black Star Square on the outskirts of the colonial Gold Coast capital at midnight on March 6, 1957, more than the the green, yellow, and red tricolor flag of independent Ghana was raised in its place. A decolonization movement arose that would soon engulf fifty-two nations and two hundred million people on the African continent alone. And more was to come. In the eyes of the African diaspora there was special meaning in the black star used atop the independence arch that dominated that parade ground and the black star emblazoned in the center of that flag. It conveyed a militant sense of independence and new hope of dignity for Africans and peoples of African descent around the globe.

The bold black star and brave new world faded quickly. Economies collapsed under the control of European buyers of cocoa or coffee, peanuts or sisal, and growing urbanization and burgeoning populations. So long as the cold war persisted and the two great powers offered these poor states the loans and military help that came from playing off one against the other, their leaders had chips. One of the ironic consequences of the great thaw in the aftermath of glasnost was that the value of Third World nations, even as pawns, in superpower conflicts was eliminated.

In the vacuum that followed, the options available to Africa's fragile regimes diminished dramatically; the Washington-based World Bank or the International Monetary Fund provided only a minimum of debt relief, and then with hefty strings attached. The political crises that followed came to be called the "democracy movement" in Africa, as one ethnic group mobilized against others and religious revivals provided reasons to take up arms against rivals in states that could no longer afford a reliable internal security system.

Observers of African politics might wonder forty years after decolonization exactly what had been accomplished by the flag-raising in Black Star Square. The internal affairs of the new states remained in local hands, but the very idea of the state has become problematical. The economies of the states remain largely in the hands of firms headquartered in the former European colonial powers. And an enormous debt to Paris, London, and Washington has now accumulated. The parts allocated by the European scriptwriters in the drama of decolonization have allowed for remarkably limited roles and a carefully circumscribed independence of action by the Third World leaders.

Charles C. Stewart

Charles Stewart

Black over White?

It was over in less than two minutes. The German, Max Schmeling, sprawled on the ropes and slumped to the canvas, defenseless. The fury, the speed, the power of the American, Joe Louis, had destroyed him.

Few boxing matches have had the promotion that this 1938 heavyweight title fight had. Two years earlier, in 1936, Schmeling had pounded Louis, imposing on the young sensation his first defeat, a knockout. Yet Louis rebounded to win the world title. In June 1938, he defended it against his nemesis. Promoters billed the Louis-Schmeling matchup as a battle between Democracy and Fascism. International politics charged the fight with unexpected excitement. Louis's stunning victory made him a compelling champion of democracy as well as an instantaneous all-American hero, one of the first African Americans to achieve that status. The moment was etched indelibly on the memory of the African diaspora. Yet the democracy Louis had defended with such muscular vitality embodied fundamental contradictions. Joe Louis was champion in a country where lynching still occurred, and where racial segregation prevailed in education, residence, health care, the armed forces, and in the national pastime, baseball. Moreover, almost all the democratic powers that Hitler threatened were also imperial powers. In decidedly undemocratic fashion, they ruled over the indigenous, nonwhite populations of Africa and Asia.

When Joe Louis died in 1981, more than forty years after his fight with Schmeling, legal segregation had ended in the United States, and affirmative action laws promoted integration in politics, education, and the workplace. Yet America remained a profoundly segregated society, a country in which race continued to govern social interactions, including those with Joe Louis. In later life, Louis was but a shell of the majestic young athlete who had taken the world by storm. He worked as a greeter at a Las Vegas casino, his fortune dissipated, his mental faculties reduced. His career was not so different from that of other African Americans of his generation—Bessie Smith, Billie Holiday—whose talents could not be denied by a society which at the same time could not fully accept them.

Radio and newspapers brought the excitement of Joe Louis's triumphs to tenements, street corners, and beer halls across the globe, to Africa and Asia as well as to Montgomery, Alabama, and Harlem. At the same time, Louis's twelve-year reign as world champion coincided with the upheavals, which, between 1947 and 1960, transformed international politics. Pride in race, nationality, and culture mobilized Third World peoples to dismantle Europe's white empires and to establish political sovereignty. Black over white prevailed throughout the colonial world, rooting out even the tenacity of apartheid in South Africa by the 1990s.

But, while the indigenous peoples of Africa and Asia had claimed political independence, they did so within a global order that shamelessly still reflected the racial hierarchy of the 1930s. Life expectancy, opportunities for education, and other indices of well-being remained largely determined by race and national origin. Political sovereignty did not automatically give people the power to improve their lives. Nation-building brought on civil conflict, famine, and genocide. And it brought a proliferation of casinos.

Donald E. Crummey

R. Azzi/Woodfin Camp

Islam

One of the most impressive moments of religious observance on the globe is the holy month of Ramadan, a time of purification and self-discipline for more than a billion Muslims. During the daylight hours of fasting their deprivation reminds believers of God's greatness. At dusk the faithful prostrate themselves in prayer, forming a global wave of worshipers beginning in the Philippines and progressing across China and Indonesia, India, southern Russia, the Middle East, and Africa. Ramadan is also a time of celebration: festive lanterns are hung in the streets, special holiday sweets are prepared, and friends and families exchange visits each evening after sunset prayer, when the fast is broken. Ramadan is observed by even the least observant; it is both an intensely spiritual and a socially solidifying experience. It renews and reinforces the human bonds that the modern age has frayed—bonds of kinship, friendship, neighborhood, and the larger religious community. In city after city, Cairo, Istanbul, Kano, and Djakarta, the prayer marking the end of Ramadan spills out of the mosque into parking lots and streets, covered with mats for the occasion. High-rise buildings, symbols of the modern business and professional classes, look down on worshipers who, in turn, cast eyes downward in humility and gratitude to God.

The century was not supposed to end like this. Even before it began Europeans heralded the advent of a secular, scientific age when religion would be consigned to history. Muslims were told that their advancement in the modern world would be delayed if they clung to superstition and faith. Yet the apostles of secularism did not reckon with human spiritual needs, nor the with the power of religions like Islam to serve those needs. They also failed to foresee the range of dynamic and creative Islamic responses to the challenges of the modern age. These responses began before the dawn of the twentieth century, when reform-minded modernist clerics in India and Egypt sought to find in religious law a way to live as a Muslim in modern society. Politically moderate and focusing their efforts on education and juridical interpretation, the modernists have largely succeeded in changing the ways in which Muslims understand and apply their holy law, the Sharia.

Another response came early in this century and outside the clerical establishment with the rise of the Muslim Brotherhood, a mass lay organization dedicated to achieving a theocratic order. Its combination of propaganda, charitable activities, and political action (including violence) remains the standard formula for militant groups from Lebanon's Hezbollah to the F.I.S. in Algeria, which thrive on economic despair, political mismanagement, and the unresolved Arab-Israeli conflict. Although these extremists monopolize the headlines, vastly larger organizations like the worldwide Tabligi Jama'at and the Muhammadiyya in Indonesia avoid politics and quietly work to improve religious education, encourage personal adherence to the holy law, and cultivate spiritual renewal.

Why, a century after its predicted withering away, does Islam continue to flourish and to appeal to such a wide variety of people? At least part of the answer is that it is many things in one: a way of life for entire communities, a faith that fulfills the spiritual and social needs of many, and for some, also, a source of political action.

Kenneth M. Cuno

The Pope in Africa

By the late nineteenth century religion in the West and Christianity in particular was on the defensive, especially among intellectuals. In this age of Darwin, Protestant theologians felt pressure to interpret Christian doctrine and to read the Bible in ways that did not seem to contradict science. Christ was seen primarily as the greatest moral teacher; the "supernatural" aspects of his divinity were strenuously played down.

After the carnage and monumental stupidity of World War I, however, faith in human rationality and progress seemed misplaced, while religion became more relevant and meaningful to thinking people in the West. Many illustrious individuals turned to religion between 1920 and 1950. The poets T. S. Eliot and W. H. Auden, the novelists Evelyn Waugh and Aldous Huxley, the Oxford professor C. S. Lewis, and the physicist Max Planck were all either converted to Catholicism or attracted to faith for the first time. Religion, often of a despairing, existential variety, was one meaningful answer to rediscovered terror and anxiety in a brutal century of war. One famous Roman Catholic convert, English novelist Graham Greene, wrote: "One began to believe in heaven because one believed in hell."

The revival of Christianity among intellectuals has been matched in recent years by a surge of popular, often fundamentalist, varieties of Christianity. At the same time, Judaism, Islam, and Hinduism have experienced similar resurgences. The enduring importance of religion in contemporary life and human thought—an importance that has often escaped historians—prompts reflection.

Pope John Paul II exemplifies several aspects of the worldwide religious revival. A jet-age evangelist, John Paul has thought and acted on a global scale. His repeated visits to distant shores have drawn large and enthusiastic crowds. In this photograph, a group of nuns radiate faith and joy as they welcome the pontiff on his tour to West Africa in 1993. The scene captures the open and international character of John Paul's Catholicism as racially integrated believers greet the "Polish Pope," including members of a Calcutta-based order founded by Mother Teresa, a Yugoslavian nun who has devoted her life to the suffering of the poor in the slums of Hindu India.

Criticized by some as an irrelevant reactionary and by others as throwback to doctrinaire Catholicism, John Paul II has in fact joined a compassionate, almost "leftist" social gospel with strict conservatism in doctrinal matters. He has advocated a more equitable distribution of income and wealth and more civil liberties, but also reaffirmed the church's long-standing opposition to contraception, abortion, and the ordination of women as priests. Pope John Paul's combination of popular and traditional captures the worldwide religious revival that has marked the last half of the twentieth century. Ordinary people everywhere are pummeled and sometimes overwhelmed by relentless change (civil war, material shortages, overcrowded cities), which has become as unpredictable as it is inexplicable. And everywhere increasing numbers seek sustenance by maintaining (or reconstructing) caring religious communities and by drawing upon spiritual beliefs with deep roots in history. Twentieth-century fates are inextricably intertwined with twentieth-century faiths.

John P. McKay

Paul Yao/Gamma Liaison

95

The Green Revolution

The Green Revolution is one of history's surprises—surprising because agrarian modernization was attempted in a century that has fervently believed in industrial development, surprising also because it succeeded so well and represented a great, though uneven, step forward for Third World peoples. The intriguing picture captures the essence of this quiet but powerful transformation of rural life. A proud owner of a two-acre plot shows a visiting expert his crop of miracle rice. Agricultural laborers stoop to do their back-breaking work under a blazing sun. And a fetosj statue designed to frighten off evil spirits stands by, suggesting that modern technology may work best when complementing cultural tradition.

For most of the twentieth century, agriculture has been largely neglected. After World War II, Third World leaders were convinced that all-out industrialization was the only answer to cruel poverty in a primitive agricultural economy. And the industrialization drive they launched was in many ways a great success. Industry grew at more than 7 percent per year in the noncommunist developing countries between 1950 and 1970, outstripping agriculture and sparking annual growth of per capita income of about 2.5 percent. Nevertheless, by the late 1960s disillusionment with the Third World's relatively rapid industrialization was spreading. The gap between the world's poor south and its rich north continued to widen. Moreover, industrialization privileged city dwellers, while peasants and rural laborers—the mass of the population—gained little or nothing.

The limitations of industrial development forced Third World governments to take a renewed interest in rural life and agricultural technology. Plant scientists and agricultural research stations had already set out to develop new hybrid seeds genetically engineered to suit the growing conditions of tropical agriculture. Their model was the extraordinarily productive hybrid corn developed for the American Midwest in the 1940s. The first breakthrough came in Mexico in the 1950s and in the 1960s an American-backed team in the Philippines developed a "miracle rice." Although the new hybrids required more fertilizer and water, they yielded more and grew much faster. They permitted the revolutionary advent of year-round farming on irrigated land, making possible two, three, or even four crops a year.

Increases in grain production were heartening and often dramatic. Across the subcontinent, Indian farmers increased production more than 60 percent in fifteen years. By 1980, thousands of new grain bins dotted the countryside, symbols of the agricultural revolution and the country's newfound ability to feed all its people. China followed with its own version of the Green Revolution under Deng Xiao-ping.

The Green Revolution was no cure-all. Experience in East Asia, the most successful region, showed that the greatest benefits went to landowners (both large and small) at the expense of tenant farmers and landless laborers. Nor has sub-Saharan Africa benefited significantly. Climatic conditions there encouraged a continuation of dry farming and root crops, whereas the Green Revolution has been almost synonymous with intensive irrigation and grain production. Nonetheless in a century that has seen so many economic catastrophes, the desert's steady advance on the sown, the Green Revolution is a heartening success story.

John P. McKay

Courtesy of the Hagley Museum and Library

Abundance

The twentieth-century global demographic explosion pales alongside the revolution in food production, transportation, and consumption during the past one hundred years. Today, the American farmer on the Internet can watch weather patterns a half a world away and adjust production and marketing strategies on a daily basis. Palm oil proteins in Indonesia do battle with soybean exports from Illinois, Russian wheat with Kansas grain, and Brazilian futures determine the price of tomorrow's baguettes in Paris and pita bread in Cairo. Agriculture goes chemical and where chemistry leaves off genetic engineering takes up. Productivity is ever more closely tied to soil additives; product color and stability is an output geared to marketability and shelf life. Pockets of global starvation at the century's end are blamed on glitches in transportation networks, not on the availability of food.

The food pictured here that would feed a North American family of four for one year in the 1950s had soared to heights unimaginable in 1900. And it has further increased in volume during the last fifty years, as it has for most families worldwide. It has also become at once more exotic and less seasonal, thanks to genetic engineering and sophisticated transportation systems. Today's Saharans buy (expensive) Macintosh apples that had never been seen by their grandparents; Canadians add tropical kiwis to their diets, and Germans, Caribbean ugli fruit that had not been known fifty years ago. We eat out and we order in. Food has become a prime example of a value-added product in our economy; and the icons of abundance now extend well beyond those 1950s frozen TV dinners to include imported pasta in Zaire, tinned tomato paste in India, and American steak and dried Romanian mushrooms in Japan.

In a global economy of abundance not only are we what we eat but our expanded waistlines testify to the fact that we have become what we have eaten. Rotundity is an inevitable sign of conspicuous consumption, even if fashion warns Rubenesque is not picturesque.

Our acts of consumption have become part of our self-stylization and it is by those acts that we judge others. Starvation in a country is a sign of political ineptitude. We glory in the underlying wonder of, perhaps divine guidance for, our abundance, if not the maladies tied to it. We are proud of our generous gifts of redundant food to thinner peoples. Supreme satisfaction can be found in the perfect meal. Abundance of food has become a global achievement not simply of the century but of all time recorded. Starvation is now a damning indictment of a global failure to provide humankind's most fundamental right.

Charles C. Stewart

UPI/Corbis-Bettmann

Suburbs

The twentieth century generated novel shapes and new meanings for everyday life. In ever more tumultuous and diverse American cities, for example, waves of immigrants mixed Old World skills and New World expectations into new experiments for collective living and provoked an endless commentary about their hopes and dissatisfactions. But these urbanites also remained in motion. They settled in the city center and cherished its exuberance, then moved on to new suburban settlements at the city's edge. From being the retreat of a privileged elite who could afford to enjoy the freshness of the village green while making a living downtown, by the 1950s the suburb had accumulated the aspirations (and car payments and mortgages) of thousands of nuclear families and forged them into an emerging mass culture.

The suburban ideal was not completely original—it re-created the housing patterns of peasant and small-town ancestors—but it did reshape the lives of the families it sheltered in important ways. Its domestic cocoon focused social activity on a narrowed family unit that supplied suburbia's main interests: marital companionship and child-focused leisure fostered through the pleasures of backyard living. Wider community and political life in the new settlements tended to serve these private aims, stripping revenue from the city that still supported them and promoting the tendency to invest politics with "family values." For many inhabitants, these values and the suburban life that expressed them fulfilled long-standing, heartfelt ambitions. The pride and privacy of a home of one's own, a lawn, a garden, a patio, and the small family circle they contained were welcome respites from the uncertainty and privation of economic depression and war. At the same time, the roles that suburbia offered remained limited. Men were breadwinners, women stay-at-home housewives with young children, a scenario that produced boredom and frustration, which have become as typically suburban as the scenes of domestic contentment.

Meanwhile, settlements on the urban periphery spoke as profoundly of the century's cruel inequalities as they did of its mass-democratic hopes. American suburbs reshaped urban racial conflict through restrictive agreements and economic requirements that hardened the territorial lines of racial division. They found their mirror images in the

UPI/Corbis-Bettmann

UPI/Corbis-Bettmann

resettlements of official racial separatism in Africa—southern African "townships"—euphemistically renamed "high density suburbs" when new majority governments inherited the housing crises born of racist development policy. And they found their antithesis in the shantytowns multiplying worldwide. There the displaced sought a homeless foothold in the same global economy that had helped create the attainable comforts of the "crabgrass frontier."

Kathryn J. Oberdeck

The Pill

The Pill is probably the only medication used worldwide without a name; it is universally known only as "the Pill." The birth control pill, first sold in 1960, is over 95 percent effective in preventing unwanted pregnancies. It is clearly a feminine object, marketed in pink or floral boxes, yet it is equally significant for men and it carries far-reaching political implications. The Pill, in short, is far more than a contraceptive: it symbolizes at once freedom and domination in the last half of the century.

The Pill has been credited with causing "the sexual revolution" in the United States. However, the increase in premarital heterosexual sex is not a recent development but a long-term twentieth-century trend. What has changed during the twentieth century are the patterns of women's sexual activity. Increasingly, women's sexual histories are more like men's: sex outside marriage and multiple partners have long been common among men; in this century they became more common among women as well. This new technology, regardless of its reputation, did not make women and men equal, however. Because the Pill nearly eliminates the fear of pregnancy, it also eliminates one traditional excuse for avoiding intercourse—the need to avoid pregnancy. Ironically, this freedom also means new pressures, both on teenage girls, for whom the Pill makes the sexual demands of boys harder to resist, and on boys to make those demands.

The Pill is associated with freedom in the West, but it has also been promoted as a primary method of population control. The product was designed in part to combat "overpopulation," which, according to its sponsors, threatened social disorder. The theory of overpopulation blamed poverty, and related social problems, on large families rather than on economic conditions. Population control programs were directed at reducing the number of poor and minority populations in the United States and in the Third World in order to prevent social revolution. The places where the Pill was initially tested in the mid-1950s—Puerto Rico, Haiti, and the poor barrios of Los Angeles—underline the assumptions of its development. Although the Pill was offered to poor women worldwide with less than their liberation in mind, it should be recognized that poor women accepted and used the Pill for their own reasons.

Despite the effectiveness of the Pill and its celebration for producing new freedom, the twentieth century has achieved neither the elimination of unwanted pregnancy nor sexual liberation for women or men.

Leslie J. Reagan

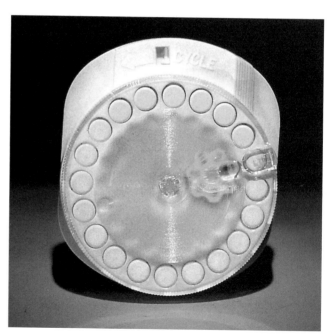

Courtesy of the Smithsonian Institution, NMAH/Medical Sciences

TV

My mother says that when she first heard about TV in the 1930s or 1940s, she imagined it would be like the movies in your living room: you would pull down a big screen, like at the cinema. In a way we did re-create—at home, cheaply and more regularly— the rare family outings to the movies that she remembered. Every Sunday night we got to stay up late for "Disney." "Ozzie and Harriet" and "The Donna Reed Show" projected the family we tried to be. Then there were the scenes about what we became—conflicts about Vietnam, about Archie Bunker, about whether wives should work. Instead of going out to relieve the stress of domestic life, we domesticated the battles of the 1960s—on TV.

That made my sister and me part of the first TV generation. Critics said because of this we lived in a vast wasteland; we found opportunities for shrewd analysis nevertheless. As teenagers, we relieved our sullen frustrations by watching detective shows together—"The Streets of San Francisco," "Kojak"—and by pretty accurately predicting the plot lines. This demonstrated, we believed, that we had not been taken in, the wasteland was not our experience. Then we went to college, graduate school—she became a television news graphics designer, I became a historian of popular culture.

Growing up in South Africa, my husband did not see television until the 1970s. The most powerful structure for organizing TV—broadcasting to a mass public—did not appeal to the architects of political and cultural apartheid, who sought to separate audiences, not unite them in a single mass. So they crafted the antithesis of television broadcasting—different channels for different languages, different races, different cultures. Defying the technology's most utopian promises—a worldwide community of culture—South Africa screened some of the century's most painful, contorted cultural divisions.

Later, in one of the century's more sublime examples of technological promises trumping grim realities, Nelson Mandela walked to freedom on TV. The world welcomed him, and he flew around to meet it. He tells of passing through Alaska and encountering some Innuit youths. "I had read about the Innuit . . . as a boy," he recalls, "and the impression I received from the racist colonialist texts was that they were a backward culture. . . . But in talking to these bright young people, I learned that they had watched my release on television and were familiar with events in South Africa. 'Viva ANC!' one of them said. What struck me so forcefully was how small the planet had become during my decades in prison; it was amazing to me that a teenaged Innuit living at the roof of the world could watch the release of a political prisoner on the southern tip of Africa. Television had shrunk the world and had in the process become a great weapon for eradicating ignorance and promoting democracy."

Even so, the grimness also continued to trump the promises. In the world of the 1990s through which Mandela traveled, cultures and nations still clashed before us, on TV. Images of South Africa reconstructing itself alternated with pictures of American soldiers headed to distant deserts and the CNN newsreels of Yugoslavia disintegrating.

Global village. Living-room war.

Kathryn J. Oberdeck

Robert Siebrecht

Wendy Stone/Gamma Liaison

Betty Press/Woodfin Camp

Marketplace

Adam Smith, the eighteenth-century moral philosopher and founding figure of modern economics, believed that human beings possessed an innate desire to buy and sell, "to truck and barter." Markets—and greedy traders—were as old as history. But Smith argued optimistically that the pursuit of narrow self-interest in competitive markets was actually the source of a previously unrecognized harmony. The "invisible hand" of competition for one and for all would thwart the schemes of selfish individuals and would-be monopolists. Free competition would provide the most effective means of increasing human wealth and well-being.

This colorful open-air market in West Africa suggests what Smith must have been thinking about. The buyers and sellers are looking for bargains and profits—not some idealistic abstraction. There are many participants and apparently few barriers to entry. Thus the combinations by traders to fix prices and eliminate competition that Smith anticipated should have only temporary success and cause little harm.

This scene also suggests how the government regulations and monopolistic privileges that Smith criticized can stifle trade and hurt the public good. When in the 1960s and 1970s many African governments imposed artificially low prices on food in order to curry favor with volatile urban populations, peasant producers responded by selling less food. Shortages invariably developed. When African governments relaxed their controls, markets like this one flourished again and shortages disappeared (except where droughts and civil wars upset market forces).

The role of markets and competition in modern history is extraordinarily complex. That complexity extends far beyond the controversies raised by those economists and statisticians who proclaim that a market economy freed of government regulations is the only path to wealth for nations. Indeed, thinking about markets has become nothing less than a pervasive discourse, a means of constructing meanings and imagining futures in the twentieth century.

This discourse has become part of everyday life. The rise of giant corporations around the late nineteenth century reopened the question of state regulation and stimulated debate on the value of "monopolistic" competition. Since the beginning of the twentieth century, regulation, deregulation, and reregulation have in turn provided a crazy quilt of conflicting blueprints, which have varied greatly by industry, nation, and time period. Similar attempts to construct meaning have marked changing visions of world trade. (In 1900 big business in the United States and the Republican party preached high tariffs as the key to strong profits and high wages, a position that their descendants dismissed as ridiculous one hundred years later.)

At the end of the century, the market perspective increasingly permeates everything from art and culture to personal relations and family life. Orchestral seasons, museum shows, and the like are consumed by audiences of customers (rather than connoisseurs) whose presence (rather than appreciation) validates the aesthetic choices of the producers. Every aesthetic sensibility has a bottom line. Market forces can also explain the fact that women working outside the home are more likely to get a divorce; the stay-at-home housewife has fewer economic opportunities and is more dependent on her husband's wages. Even our most basic orientations are structured by markets. Just think of the expression "it pays." For example, those who pray regularly have better health and fewer medical expenses, so "prayer pays." The imperialism of market thinking marches on, having shaped the twentieth century more profoundly than any other.

John P. McKay

Airplane Eye

The earth has never looked so strange as when seen from the air. Distinctly twentieth-century perspectives reveal a totally built landscape that serves as a spur to technocratic ambitions for the colonization of the natural world. By the end of the century, wild land is mostly preserved as parkland, genes are mapped and manipulated, and "high-tech" solutions are found to repair human biology and ecological degradation. Is not clear whether the "natural" can be disentangled from the "artificial." The globe appears more and more as a huge Faustian workshop, expanding, connecting, and illuminating, and finally throwing its products into space.

Aerial views do not show distinct snapshots of fields or factories. Sprawling cities no longer terrorize fields and woods and villages, but constitute one element in a checkered modernist abstract. Urban grays merge with agrarian browns and rural greens and yellows. Only by airplane is it possible to discover the rational design of the city, to pull together in a single view its endless roadways and boulevards, or to appreciate the ceaseless construction in the suburbs. Soot, grime, and noise on the ground are transformed into a luminous sea of houses arranged according to a previously unsuspected order. In much the same way, nature's green-dented ground appears to be tidily laced with railroad tracks, highways, and field boundaries. From the air, the countryside resembles a vast and fabulous product: a tablework checkered, parceled, and sliced by a modernist geometry.

"L'avion accuse"—with this rallying cry the modernist Le Corbusier indicted Europe's old cities after World War I. It was the "airplane eye," Le Corbusier claimed, that had brought the failure of the unplanned city to light. The "spectacle of collapse" in Paris, London, and Berlin was clearly visible from the air. Sheafs of aerial photographs showed a helter-skelter disarray of "small plots . . . small doors . . . streets in sinister confusion, full of noise and squalor." All this had to be torn down and rebuilt in more functional fashion.

But for Le Corbusier, the "airplane eye" also served as an agent of reform. He was astonished at how plastic and malleable to human touch the earth's surface appeared from the air. A bird's-eye perspective encouraged more central and rational planning. The perspective of the machine would overcome narrow interests and adhere to principles that were "sane, clear-headed, logical, harmonious and beautiful." This modernist clarity Le Corbusier celebrated not only for the salutary social reform it permitted but also for the part it played in restoring purpose and direction to public affairs. Full of breathless enthusiasm for Mussolini, Le Corbusier announced the necessity of "a man!" who would reveal "the power of genius" and serve as shepherd for the century's wayward flock. Technology and command went hand in hand.

In the United States, cultural critics such as Stuart Chase and Lewis Mumford argued much the same thing. The aviator's "celestial eyesight" dramatized the depression-era wreckage of industrial America. Cities were overly large and too disconnected from transportation routes and raw materials. Mumford foresaw far-reaching electrical corridors and airline networks which would untie settlements from intersections of roads and railways and permit the dispersal of the city onto the countryside, a "fourth migration" that is plainly depicted by this satellite photograph of the industrial glow of the United States in the 1980s. Spread out like a huge map, the world below the pilot conformed to its manufactured representation.

Peter Fritzsche

108

Machines and Work

The century sprang to life amidst a second industrial revolution—electricity and internal combustion replaced steam, high speed steel and rayon replaced iron and cotton, scientific management with its personnel and production specialists replaced the drive system and its powerful foreman. Millions still toiled in small shops, but the giant factory—U.S. Steel and International Harvester, Krupp and Seimens—became an icon of the era. Towering turbines and cavernous blast furnaces harnessed enormous energy, dwarfing the workers servicing them. Yet with all the new machinery, the worker was everywhere. The symmetry of the industrial economy, like the aesthetic in the photograph, was created by the combination of the giant machine with the strength of the worker.

The century ends with another great burst of technical and management innovation—the age of the smart machine. In between, mechanization and higher productivity have come in great bursts—in the 1920s, during the two world wars, and with "automation" in the 1950s. Although the term "automation"—the direct displacement of human by machine labor—has been employed at least since the third decade of this century, most changes in work during our century have come through the sort of increasingly minute division of work that Adam Smith first observed in an eighteenth-century Birmingham pin factory or through new tools, fab-

Courtesy George Eastman House

IBM Archives

rics, and power sources. Only in the past generation have robots taken over specific production tasks on assembly lines, although the worker remains somewhere in the mix. In the photo, the worker seems almost overwhelmed by the computer control board, but if the machine is really on its own, then what is he doing inside there?

In science fiction new technology and the resulting transformation of occupations have often been sources for a new life of leisure. In reality, along with the downward pressures of global labor and commodity markets and ag-gressive new management strategies, they have often brought a significant intensification of work. The same forces seem to be reducing the value of human labor and breaking any remaining control industrial workers exert over production. Yet the very sophistication and intricacy of com-puter technology can render modern workplaces peculiarly vulnerable, and workers are already exploiting this vul-nerability in conflicts with management over wages, hours, and other issues that are far older than the century.

Few elements of life have changed more in this century than work; yet aspects of the experience seem almost timeless. At the birth of the computer age, hundreds of millions still toil with their hands in dismal settings through-out the world. Hundreds of millions more work with sophisticated machin-ery in sterile plants, for low wages, often facing frightening health hazards. At the century's end, technology re-mains more servant than master, its distribution and application still reflecting the power relations of the societies that produce it and control it.

James R. Barrett

Plastics

The history of the twentieth century lies in heaps of rubbish. Archeologists excavate garbage or pits to tell us about ancient societies; future archeologists will explore our garbage and come away impressed by our reliance on plastics. Long after the rest of our garbage has been transformed into dirt, plastic will retain its shape, testifying to the extraordinary wastefulness and the unexpected resilience of modern times.

Plastic is a petroleum product, but not one of the great oil barons of the turn of the last century could have predicted either the staggering range of things that the industrialized world manufactures from petroleum or the sheer disposability (and indestructibility) of those products. Since the 1960s, most plastics are disposables: wrappers, diapers, trays, syringes, and the like. Every medical consultation or dental examination involves a pair of disposable plastic gloves. In the rich West, these disposables are burned or simply thrown into landfills or into oceans. Much of the world's population uses plastic very differently, however. In the shantytowns of Africa, Asia, and Latin America, plastic bags and sheeting are building materials for houses; syringes are used and reused (at least where medicines are available); and pesticide canisters reappear in markets as measuring ladles for grain.

It is the West, then, that must confront the problem of disposability. Burying plastic garbage works fine, but nobody wants a rubbish heap next door. Burning disposables releases air- and water-born carcinogens. The toxicity that results affects not just us and our children but also the plants and animals around us. The survival of the bald eagle is imperiled by water-born toxins; beluga whales in the estuary of the St. Lawrence River suffer from lung disease and cancer, the victims of industrial pollutants pumped into Lake Ontario and carried downriver by eels; black-footed albatrosses, which breed far out in the north Pacific on Midway atoll, are afflicted by reproductive disorders caused by toxic pollutants born by ocean currents from the trash dumps of the Pacific Rim.

Yet nature is strangely adaptable and resilient. In this photograph gulls wheel and soar. Within the garbage heaps, tiny microbes flourish. In the Northeast and Midwest of the United States, suburbs have become fresh habitats for raccoons, possums, and skunks. Thanks to leash laws, hunting regulations, and the elimination of wolves, whitetail deer have multiplied prodigiously in many parts of the eastern United States. Plastic garbage attests to new, often disastrous, and occasionally unexpected relations between humans and animals. One thing is clear at the end of the century that was not understood in 1900: we cannot conquer nature, only cooperate with it.

Donald E. Crummey

Refugees

Mother, daughter, granddaughter. Hurrying, cold, anguished faces. How many times has this scene been replayed in our century, the century of displacement and dispossession? The century of refugees. This image happens to show a family of Kurdish refugees, but their expressions might as easily have come from the faces of Armenians, Jews, Vietnamese, or Rwandans. A by-product of this century's nationalist and totalitarian ideologies, advanced weaponry, and total war has been the repeated uprooting and exile of populations on a vast scale. On a much smaller scale have been efforts to develop effective machinery to deal with refugees because of political rivalries and the reluctance of states to cede sovereignty.

More than anything else, wars create refugees. World War I produced nearly four million refugees; World War II uprooted more than ten times as many people. Third World conflicts, especially in the post–cold war era since 1989, have reaped a third and equally impressive wave of refugees. In the early 1990s there were an estimated forty million international refugees and internally displaced persons, more than half of whom were in Asia, the Middle East, Africa, and Central America. Refugee stories now make up a regular feature of the evening news in Johannesburg and Chicago, Manila and Dakar. Only the most privileged of us can resolve the problem by switching channels; among the majority are people who live daily in the shadow of haunting despair, of displacement. Mother, daughter, grandchild; hurrying, cold, anguished faces. Icons to involuntary population movement at the end of the century.

Kenneth M. Cuno

Teit Hornbak 2 Maj/Impact Visuals

Counterculture

While stimulating and satisfying material desires at an increasing rate and putting commodities in wide if unequal circulation, the twentieth century also inherited ethical traditions that placed wisdom beyond the empire of tangible goods. Ralph Waldo Emerson's lament that "Things are in the saddle and ride mankind" and Henry David Thoreau's motto "That man is the richest whose pleasures are the cheapest" have continued to echo among seekers after transcendent self-knowledge who were concerned about a society grown too complacent, too soft, too unreflective. Yet the search for authentic selfhood became ever more elusive as metaphysical speculations found an expanding market of their own. Over the radio, between commercials, evangelists peddled ever sterner versions of the "Good Word" while bookstores offered pricey guides to "Eastern religion" and spirituality. This courtship between the spiritual and the commercial was hardly new, but in the 1960s it became more intense than ever in the "counterculture" that briefly flourished among youth in the industrialized West.

Amidst a material abundance their parents had only dreamed of in youth, a small army of spiritual seekers sought to reenchant the world. They rejected the dress of corporate office for the denim and flannel which they associated with the noble simplicity of the dispossessed. They scorned individual ambition in favor of ritualized community. And they overturned routine with mind-altering drugs and celebratory music, "turned on, tuned in, dropped out" in pursuit of deeper meaning and an inner light. Cynics dismissed such alternatives to the modern world as pipe dreams and critics noted their bleaker moments of self-deception and exploitation. Still, in its more visionary phases, the counterculture expressed a powerful hunger for selfhood and community not calibrated to profit or prestige. Its cultural monuments—like the music festival at Woodstock—prophesied a new age of long-haired, flower-powered friends liberated to do what they wanted.

The troubling irony in all this beamed from the billboards and boutiques that hawked the stuff of cultural rebellion. Nonconformity could be packaged and sold as easily as anything else, and advertisers were keen manipulators of the very images that indicted their market motives. A "prophetic minority" more active in politics than poetry wrestled with these contradictions in the culture of rebellion, but the capacity of the market to capture and co-opt antimaterialist aspirations remains overwhelming. These dilemmas of abundance are rare enough in a world of want. But they pose another kind of poverty for those who seek their own Waldens for spiritual sustenance and find only Wal-Marts on the edge of town.

Kathryn J. Oberdeck

117

Jukebox

Rock 'n' roll is just another word for autobiography, at least for baby boomers. Out of album cuts and radio jingles, I used to construct my own soundtrack that I played and spliced to suit the adventures of growing up. Intensely personal—self-indulgent, sometimes vulgar, and occasionally embarrassing—my jukebox memory is stirred whenever I spin the dial to the "Golden Oldies" station.

"Games People Play," The Spinners. We talked for hours at a time about girls as we drove aimlessly in Jon's car, listening to FM radio, sometimes going as far as Jana's house in South Shore, wondering which of us she might be thinking about. It was 1975, a year when a few of my friends had their drivers' licenses, but well before the age of sneaking into the local pubs for beers. The most important song on our winter drives was "Games People Play." We searched the radio over and over again for that song. To hear it play was like suddenly finding your way out of the labyrinth, feeling intimately connected to power and possibility. Jana was sure to be thinking of me now. The surest sign of adolescent grace was to predict that "Games People Play" was going to be the next song. One night I called it right and really thought I might be able to call them all. I was keyed in, until the next time I tried.

"Reasons," Earth, Wind, and Fire. Once we learned to dance, "Reasons," sung by Maurice White, became our favorite. If you couldn't kiss a girl during "Reasons," it wasn't going to happen. When Hank returned from France that same summer, he taught us the latest disco dances. Jumpy and fun, they retrieved "touchdancing" and renewed interest in school dances by boys and girls, blacks and whites. I never could understand the guys that just played air guitar or people who preferred The Eagles or Elton John (although I did go out with Maria, who liked those groups, but she was still a kid).

"Close to the Edge," Yes. Nighttime was for dancing—afternoons were for lying around in Matt's basement watching James Coburn movies and listening to Yes. "Close to the Edge" is the sound of close to being in love. It became my song because Gwen liked it and when we became a couple in February 1976 she wrote down some of the words for me. That gave them obvious talismanic powers. "Close to the Edge" is the one thing I stole from our high school library; I still have the album, affixed with the school sticker and call number (A 78-S).

"There's a Thorn Tree in the Garden," Eric Clapton. If Yes didn't get us close enough to the edge, we'd put on Eric Clapton's *Layla*. This was a boy thing. Matt and I would sit in those two black leather chairs in front of the pool table and once we had talked ourselves into total melancholy, he'd put on "Layla" and then "There's a Thorn Tree in the Garden," a song I still associate with trying to be sad, a skill that any good jukebox can hone.

"I Met Him on a Sunday," Laura Nyro. Sitting in Erica's apartment in New York on 123d Street, I felt grown up. I was at Penn, she was at Columbia. We had been high-school friends, and occasionally I would visit. We'd talk all afternoon, then have dinner at an Indian restaurant on the Lower East Side. Enchanted with a city she never again left, Erica was having a much better time in college than I. And while she had grown up with all our mythology of Earth, Wind, and Fire, Erica was now listening to new sounds and having new adventures. A little bit of her city rubbed off on me.

"Light My Fire," The Doors. The driving sound and urgent, angry words make me like this song. 6:50 minutes long, it is an anthem of defiance. When Liz broke up with me in May 1980, I played it over and over again, at six in the morning, feeling furious yet strong. We later got back together before splitting up again, but it is by the break-up song that I still remember Liz.

"Rock Lobster," B-52s. I still hated college, which I suppose is the fate of people who loved high school. But in the last semester I finally fell in with a great crowd, known by its demographic: "Off Campus, Catholic, Cocaine." I wasn't Catholic, didn't do much cocaine, having made the switch to beer long before, but in our off-campus apartments (4303 Baltimore), Nina, Karen, Mark, and all the rest made up a wild group amidst a campus of would-be accountants, dentists, and what I deemed other improbable professions. When we graduated, we had the best party in the world (a Sunday in April 1980) and partied all night long, dancing to The Specials, The Talking Heads, and the B-52s, and especially to "Rock Lobster" a song which prompted us to huddle together, scream, and land on the floor.

"Brown-Eyed Girl," Van Morrison. 169 on the jukebox at The Tavern on 44th and Spruce. Best song, great bar.

Peter Fritzsche

Kung Fu Films

Bruce Lee. Jackie Chan. These two names summon up a new cinematic genre, the kung fu film. Made possible by the globalization of both cultural production and culture consumption in the late twentieth century, the kung fu film was developed in Hong Kong in the early 1970s, inspired by generic stylistic elements from Hollywood, and has remained immensely popular around the world ever since.

Kung fu is simply the Cantonese term for martial arts. Etymologically, *kung fu* means hard work, stringent discipline, and will power. It connotes the almost sadomasochistic commitment to actualizing one's entire being. The Chinese have been practicing kung fu as a means for self-defense and as a technique for self-empowerment since ancient times. But it was only in the nineteenth century, when China came to be dominated by various European empires, that kung fu took on symbolic significance of national essence, a distinctly Chinese tradition to be cultivated in order to protect the nation against foreign infringement.

This symbolic meaning played out in the films of Bruce Lee. Lee was born in San Francisco and raised in Hong Kong. He had become a popular child star before he returned to the United States at eighteen for university studies. Physically small and ethnically alien, he experienced racism. He reacted by driving himself hard to succeed. He worked maniacally on his kung fu, which he had learnt since his teens. Hoping to make his name in Hollywood, he managed to find only a few bit-parts and minor roles.

Bruce Lee eventually returned to Hong Kong in 1971 and began to make kung fu films, a powerful medium which allowed him to express his physical prowess and his feeling of racial and personal frustration. In less than two years, he had made himself into Asia's first world-class superstar and transformed the kung fu film into a global phenomenon that was particularly popular among Third World audiences. In his early films, including *Fist of Fury* (1972) and *The Way of the Dragon* (1972), Lee manages to "stage" his wrath deliberately. After suffering many humiliations, Lee waits until the climactic final scene to explode into a "total fighting machine." With his stunning physique, masculine charisma, and an eruption of shouts and shrieks, the kung fu master single-handedly destroys all his enemies, who are mostly foreigners—Japanese or Americans (including Chuck Norris and Kareem Abdul-Jabbar). In the 1970s, when Hong Kong was still economically and politically peripheral in the world order, the audiences could easily identify with and feel empowered by Lee's nationalist heroism.

Courtesy of the Academy of Motion Picture Arts and Sciences

Bruce Lee emerged as a symbol of underdog heroism. He became immensely popular in the United States, where urban audiences found his films both "pure visual and aural spectacles" and allegories of "class revenge." (But his kung fu films have also contributed to the American stereotypes of Asians as violent and vicious.) After Bruce Lee's mysterious death in 1973, it took the Hong Kong film industry several years before it found a replacement in kung fu superstar Jackie Chan. But Chan is a different character altogether. Partly the result of cinematic fashions and partly the result of Asia's achieved economic affluence, Jackie Chan's kung fu films no longer feature the romantic hero but combine fistfights with more comic gestures. Now, instead of taking revenge against foreigners, the kung fu films celebrate racial harmony and showcase Asian financial power in competition with Hollywood. Jackie Chan's films are also big-budget spectacles packed with astonishing stunts and carefully choreographed body movements. Not surprisingly, Chan's movies have become enormous blockbusters in Asia and, since 1995, in the United States.

The improbable success of the kung fu film attests to the transnational forces that shape national cultures for a global capitalist market in the late twentieth century. At the same time, the development of the genre projects Asia's economic and social achievement.

Poshek Fu

Courtesy of the Academy of Motion Picture Arts and Sciences

Tokyo

The twentieth century can be best experienced by strolling down the streets of a major city in East Asia. Nowhere are the cultural commodities promised by urban concentration as widely available, and available with such cleanliness and order and personal safety as in Tokyo, Singapore, Hong Kong. Take this narrow alley in the night through one of Tokyo's most enticing neighborhoods. Forgo the geisha, sake, and sashimi, if you wish, and drop into this baa (bar) where the hosutesu (hostess) will bring you uisukii (whiskey). White Horse or Suntory, it is all there for a price. Afterwards, why not see the latest American movie? Tomorrow, will it be tandoori or tofu? How pleasant to mull it over on the train ride home. And if you miss the last train home, there are taxis aplenty, and no fear of muggings for you or the driver. Here, in the great cities of East Asia, the aspirations of nineteenth-century London and Paris have been realized, but with the twentieth century's greater variety of cultures, commodities, and fun.

The city arose with civilization in the ancient world, and in a remarkable way one can trace the history and power of many states through shifts in urban power. Long before Athens and Rome, Babylon, Memphis, Mohenjo-Daro, Yin, and other Shang capitals were all great urban centers with considerable sophistication and regional influence. All the great urban centers of ancient civilization lay outside the West (with the possible exception of Crete). And after the fall of Rome, the great cities of the world were again in the East: Byzantium, Ghazni, Changan, and Edo. Only with the emergence of Italian city-states like Venice and Genoa at the end of the Middle Ages did the city return to Europe in a significant way. London pioneered a new concept of the modern city in the eighteenth century, a place of urban culture that depended not so much on size (Edo was larger) but on pretensions and power. This modern sense of the city as cultural center was best embodied in Paris, the cultural capital of the nineteenth century, even as fin-de-siècle Vienna and Weimar Berlin made their own assertions.

As the twentieth century now draws to a close, the city as the site of cultural and commercial power seems to have returned to East Asia. Early in the twentieth century, people sailed into "Tokio" and then Shanghai from around the world to experience the cultural hodgepodge of the modern East Asian city. With economic development during the postwar years, this experience is now available with variations on the motif in Seoul, Canton, Hong Kong, Singapore and elsewhere in East Asia. Yet, Tokyo may still be the most resilient and vibrant city in the world. Almost destroyed by the great Kanto earthquake in 1923, and bombed flat during World War II, Tokyo illustrates how the city, as well individuals, must continually reinvent itself to survive the changing demands of the twentieth century. Will the modern city survive into the next century? There is no better place to wait and see than from a window seat in a Tokyo coffee shop.

Kevin M. Doak

Jean-Marc Giboux/Gamma Liaison

124

Creating Race

Race and ethnicity are all-consuming issues in our century. In particular, race dominates contemporary political discourse in the United States, a nation of immigrants which prides itself on being the most civil, most plural, and most prosperous country in the world. Burdened by the long, painful legacy of slavery and often violent white-against-black discrimination, race matters in America. It threatens the very fundamentals of America's multicultural promise.

The identity of Asian American provides a good example. Discussions of race in the United States are cast in such black-and-white terms that Asian Americans have come to be either white, if not superwhite, regarded as a model minority in the popular press, or simply invisible. To be Asian in America is a racialized, tribalized experience rarely shared by other racial and ethnic groups.

Even to be recognized and seen as an Asian is to be regarded in completely artificially racial terms. To be an Asian makes sense only outside of Asia. On the continent itself, people identify themselves in terms of their ethnicity or nationality: Chinese, Japanese, Koreans, or Indians. They become "Asians" only after coming to the United States, which officially classifies and unofficially treats them as such. Most first-generation Asian Americans are pulled between their own (pre-American) ethnic selves and their newly acquired (American) racial identities. The extreme cultural diversity of Asia and the legacy of Japanese imperialism makes it all the more difficult for them to adopt a pan-Asian identity. For second- and third-generation Asian Americans, on the other hand, the college campus has created a place to explore and reconstruct their racial and personal identities. In order to mobilize Asians to resist anti-Asian racism and to debunk crude stereotypes, pan-Asian clubs have formed at many American universities. Inspired by the struggles of African Americans and Latino/as, they have demanded the creation of Asian American programs and more attention to America's Asian communities. Some also link their cultural politics to a broader critique of global capitalism.

There are also critics from within the Asian American community who warn against the tactics of confrontation and encourage assimilation. They point to the extreme heterogeneity of both the Asian and the wider American communities. And they argue that the only possible way for self-empowerment is to assimilate into mainstream America through education and entrepreneurship. Nonetheless, Asians know from their own experience that their body and their name, unlike those of Irish Americans or Italian Americans, have racialized, minoritized, and tribalized them no matter how "American" they actually are.

Taken on a Los Angeles street during the 1992 riots, the photograph reveals some of the anger and alienation of being marginalized in the public sphere while at the same time being projected as somehow "superwhite." The basic dilemma facing the Asian American at the end of the century is: how to be Asian without becoming "Asian."

Poshek Fu

Alexandra Avakian/PNI

126

End of Communism

The Communist century began with the stunning October 1917 Russian Revolution, the outcome of years of political turmoil. The upheavals of World War II placed the challenge of Communism squarely on the political agenda of the rest of the world, as the aptly named iron curtain fell first on Eastern Europe and China, later on Indochina, Cuba, and across parts of Africa. For four decades the world considered itself divided into (choose your own terms) free and unfree, socialist and capitalist, progressive and imperialist.

Even though observers rightly noted that Communism was wracked by enormous internal contradictions, it was hard to imagine how the Soviet Union would ever go away. It was, as Churchill put it, a "riddle wrapped in a mystery inside an enigma," apparently as impervious to change as it was to comprehension. The combination of one-party rule and control of information, military force, provision of social benefits, and national pride would likely keep the Union of Soviet Socialist Republics impoverished but intact into the twenty-first century.

Then in 1985 Mikhail Gorbachev came to power. He knew Communism needed reform, and he invited discussions on democratizing the party and modernizing the economy. His calls for reform fell on deaf ears among the Communist party leaders in the east bloc, but in 1989 the people of Eastern Europe responded enthusiastically to Gorbachev's invitation for change. First in Poland, then in Hungary, East Germany, and Czechoslovakia, and then in the Baltic republics of the USSR, popular pressure swept the Communist leaders away. Not surprisingly, Gorbachev found himself condemned by his own party for "losing" the Soviet empire and savaged by his citizens for the economic inequities his reforms had caused. In August 1991, hardliners attempted to overthrow Gorbachev and restore old-style Communism, but popular resistance and repugnance toward the party defeated the coup d'état in a matter of days.

The failed coup was the coup de grace for the Soviet Communist Party. It was not long before the Communist party was declared illegal and stripped of its possessions and prestige. One by one, its most treasured symbols were discarded. Ruby-red stars and hammers and sickles came down from their Kremlin spires, replaced by gilded double-headed eagles and glittering Orthodox crosses. The red banner of socialism was painted over with the white, blue, and red flag of prerevolutionary Russia. Jubilant crowds pulled down the once-revered statues of Lenin.

Of course it is easier to take down symbols than to dismantle systems. Once before, in 1917, revolutionaries had pulled down the old icons of the imperial order, without creating a workable socialist society. Lenin is shattered, Leninism is ignored, but the wrenching transition from a planned economy to market capitalism, from an all-inclusive social welfare system to the anarchy of laissez-faire, from the status of superpower to bit player on the world political stage has created enormous political dislocation. In fact, the red banner of Communism has returned to many provincial villages and towns. The golden arches of McDonalds and ubiquitous billboards that equate utopia with American cigarettes provide scant compensation for the loss of the ideals and the relative security of the socialist system. As the century ends, many voters wondered whether exchanging Lenin for Marlboros was really such a breath of fresh air after all.

Diane P. Koenker

Human Rights

Since 1945, discussions about human rights have dominated international affairs. At issue is how rights that are presumed to be universal and inalienable are to be defined and implemented in a diverse and increasingly "multicentric" world.

Since the end of the cold war, the tense "proxy" confrontations between the two superpowers have given way to various ethnic and regional conflicts. The debate between Asia and the West on human rights has figured as an important component in these newly revived regional differences. Some Asian countries such as China, Malaysia, and Singapore have achieved remarkable economic success toward the close of the century, and yet they continue to be subjected to almost constant criticism by the United States and its European allies because of their human rights violations. The most dramatic example was the massacre of prodemocracy protesters at Tiananmen Square in June 1989. In response, increasingly assertive Asian governments have accused the United States of using human rights as an ideological weapon to infringe on their national sovereignty and to promote its own economic agenda in the Pacific. The most outspoken of these Asian leaders, notably Singapore's former prime minister, Lee Kwan Yew, has taken the lead in trying to create ethnic and regional identities in Asia by propagating an alternative "Asian view" and specifically an "Asian democracy."

This polarization of the world into the East and West is in fundamental ways a result of centuries of Western imperialism. Postcolonial countries in Asia have been struggling to catch up with "modern" ideals. Not surprisingly, they interpret the West's attention on human rights as rooted in a lingering "Orientalist" perception of Asia as uncivilized and underdeveloped, the

region's undeniable economic successes notwithstanding. In other words, from this Asian perspective, the global distribution of power and status remains unjust.

It is in this context that we can read the Bangkok Declaration of March 1993 as an attempt by the Asian governments to empower themselves in order both to urge the Western powers to take Asia

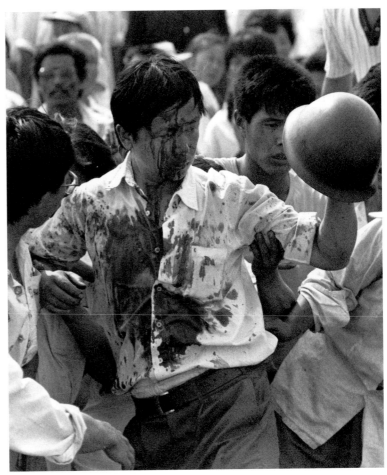

Reuters/Corbis-Bettmann

seriously and to resist the imposition of Western values and agendas in a post-colonial world order. Thus, while the document affirms universal human rights, it reshuffles these issues to privilege national sovereignty, economic stages of development, and cultural uniqueness (in the form of the "Asian Way").

Asian challenges have put the double standards of the West in relief. And yet the Bangkok Declaration reveals its own hypocrisy and problems: it does not mean that Chinese dissident Wei Jingsheng or Burma's Nobel Peace Prize winner Aung Saan Soo Kyi or Singaporean writer Gopal Baratham endure their torments for their brave voices against injustice with any less pain because they are "uniquely Asians." At the end of the century, a global public sphere appears to be emerging in which nations, races, and different ethnic constructions are using the same vocabulary and are striving to participate as equals. This development, unimaginable one hundred years ago, may be one of this century's greatest legacies.

Poshek Fu

Reuters/Arthur Tsang/Archive Photos

130

Behind the Veil

Cairo, 1987. The young woman had come to my office to discuss a term paper on the beginnings of feminism in her country.

A century ago the founders of the women's movements in Egypt, Turkey, and other Muslim countries prioritized educating women, securing their right to work outside the home, and protecting their legal rights within the family. These women did not criticize the veil, in part because it enabled them to move about in public space. Then, much as now, the discourse on veiling has been dominated by male voices. The first criticisms of the veil were launched by men who denounced it as an anachronism and who championed the "emancipation" of women as a necessary step in the advancement of the nation. Other men rose to defend veiling on the grounds of public morality and cultural authenticity. In short, the veil became elevated to a cultural symbol standing somewhat apart from issues of women's rights. It was either anachronistic or authentic, and attacking it was either progressive or mindlessly Westernist, but men and women could and did defend the veil without opposing women's rights.

The related customs of veiling and female seclusion were pre-Islamic, and were practiced in Muslim society mainly among the urban upper classes, the very classes that produced the first Muslim feminists in the late nineteenth century. Beginning in the 1920s, the old system of seclusion and veiling was abandoned, except in a handful of countries like Saudi Arabia where legal means enforced the custom. By the latter half of the century, even where veiling remained the norm, women had made important advances in education, entered the wage workforce, and took their place in formerly all-male professions. The new veiling began in the 1970s among middle-class university students—those who had benefited most from the women's rights movement—and then spread to the workplace and the public schools.

My student was veiled: the hem of her dress brushed the tops of her shoes, her sleeves came to her wrists, and her hair and neck were covered, like the San Diego middle school student pictured here, in a science class sketching trees.

That modern, educated women would voluntarily take the veil has confounded outside observers who equate it with women's oppression and see it as symptomatic of a rejection of modernity. There have even been attempts to measure the strength of fundamentalism by standing on a street corner in Cairo or Amman and counting the veiled women.

What is really behind the veil? The women who veil insist that it should be voluntary, and that they have neither returned to seclusion nor retreated from the workplace. In a society in flux the new veil is an assertion of religious and cultural identity, piety, and modesty, as well as of educational and class status. Men tend to see the veil differently. For them it is meant to cover much larger social and cultural issues. Some have proposed laws requiring women to veil and encouraging married women to remain at home, to strengthen morality and the family. Unveiled as well as veiled women have resisted these attempts to deprive them of their personal freedom.

Our conversation moved from the past to the present and the personal. How did these issues impact the life of my student? "Of course I want marry and have children, and my family will always come first," she said. "But no one is going to keep me from using my education."

Kenneth M. Cuno

Redrawing the Globe

Three times during the twentieth century, the globe had abruptly to be put back on its axis and the map of the world had to be redrawn and relabeled—in 1918–21, in 1945–47, and again in 1989–91. (A fourth process of global reordering, the dissolution of Europe's overseas empires, took place more gradually between the late 1940s and the late 1960s.) The globe may look solid, but its political surface has been periodically disassembled and rearranged.

At the end of World War I, four nineteenth-century empires collapsed with dramatic suddenness—the Russian, the Austrian, the German, and the Ottoman. A tsar and his family were murdered, and two emperors and a sultan were driven into exile. A host of new states were created or resuscitated in Eastern Europe and in the Middle East. They included Finland, Lithuania, Latvia, Estonia, Poland, Czechoslovakia, Hungary, Yugoslavia, Syria, Lebanon, Palestine, Jordan, and Saudi Arabia. Maps were also redrawn in parts of Africa and in Polynesia as German's overseas possessions were partitioned among the victors of the war.

A more abrupt and traumatic process of remapping took place a generation later in the early 1940s, when Nazi Germany conquered and re-ordered much of Europe and when Imperial Japan imposed its "co-prosperity sphere" on much of Eastern Asia and the islands of the South Pacific. Although both the German and the Japanese empires collapsed in defeat in 1945, the states of Eastern Europe that the Soviet army had "liberated" from German rule were to fall behind an "Iron Curtain" that was not to be torn down for more than four decades.

World War II served as a catalyst also for a more gradual process of imperial devolution that in the course of the late 1940s was to end British colonial rule

Gildo Nicolo Spadoni/Graphistock

in India and Dutch colonial rule in Indonesia. A decade later, a comparable process was to take place in most of French, Belgian, and British Africa as well as in the West Indies, Southeast Asia, and the Pacific. Most such changes in ultimate sovereignty meant an alteration in political authority and in name rather than the actual redrawing of territorial boundary lines.

Finally, a comparable alteration in the shape of the world occurred during the years 1989–91 as the states of Eastern Europe freed themselves from Soviet domination and as the sixteen republics—of which Russia was by far the largest—that had constituted the seventy-year-old Soviet Union broke apart. Earlier creations such as Czechoslovakia and Yugoslavia unraveled as well.

Looked at from the vantage point of the moon, the oceans and continents of the earth may appear unchanging, but one of the defining themes of the twentieth century has been the political will that—whether by the sword or by persuasion—has enabled states and peoples to draw and redraw the map of the world.

Walter L. Arnstein

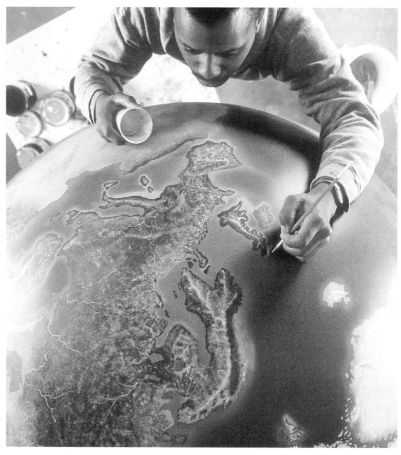

David Joel/Tony Stone

Lost Patriots

Born in 1923 into a military lineage stretching back to Napoleon and sprinkled with generals, he was sent to spend summers with his uncle, a governor, in Algeria to be exposed to the exotic yet firm French soil across the Mediterranean. During World War II, in his late teens, he hid much of the time in the forests of occupied France, working with the resistance, and for his efforts he was severely wounded by shrapnel he still carries with him. When the war concluded he was predestined to follow in the footsteps of his father and his father's father, and his military career took him first to Indochina. He was there at the time of Dien Bien Phu, and came home shortly after the 1954 Geneva settlement that divided Indochina into a Communist north and a French-supported south. His next assignment: a command post with Arab troops in Algeria. His very promising military career in defense of the disintegrating empire was cut short by a crisis at home that required his premature retirement at the age of thirty-eight, a short career that had witnessed the collapse of French control over two of her most significant overseas territories. His subsequent civilian career concluded, after retirement, as a part-time consultant to the Communist mayor of his town in a decaying industrial region of central France.

The idealism of his youth led this child of the early 1940s into the first wave of militant activism in South Africa when the African National Congress was reviving its youth league in opposition to the nationalist government's 1948 declaration of "separate but equal" policy, better known as apartheid. He was hunted by the dreaded security police soon after leaving high school and forced into exile by 1960, first in neighboring Botswana. From there his peripatetic career took him for training in Tanzania, then to Minsk in the Soviet Union; by the late 1960s he was enrolled as an undergraduate at Ethiopia's Addis Ababa University. A branded danger to South African security and unable to return home, he taught in Uganda and Kenya before going to a midwestern university in the United States for a M.A. degree in the mid-1970s. He returned first to East Africa but then went back home to see his mother as the winds of change finally began blowing through South Africa in the early 1980s. There he settled down as a teacher, then secondary school principal, but took leave to return to America in 1990 to begin a doctoral degree, since completed, with which he earned a lectureship in a university at home. His friends from high school days who stayed behind are much better placed in the majority-governed South Africa than those of his generation who lived in exile.

These two lives, each bridging the cataclysmic event of their generations—World War II and the loss of empire in one case, militant resistance and prolonged exile in the cause of fighting apartheid in the other—appear at first glance in opposition. Yet they both speak to a twentieth-century phenomena of patriots without honor. It is easy to sympathize with the soldiers pressed into the service for the glory of colonial empires during the first quarter of the century, a glory turned burden by mid-century, and a burden turned embarrassment in the third quarter of the century. It is noble to extol the heroism of the colonial freedom fighter, the liberation struggle for those who took on those soldiers and were incarcerated or exiled for their efforts. But what happened when they came out of the forest? What became of the Vietnam veterans (on both sides), the combatants in the Mau Mau events in Kenya (on both sides), the Russian veterans from Afghanistan and F.L.N. exiles from Algeria? The pattern across all these good causes is one of patriots who find advantage has passed to the ones who stayed home. The cause for which they fought may be over, sometimes even won, but their personal

La Photographie, Montluçon, France

stake has been eclipsed by other events.

It may be a sign of weak ideology propping up the nation-state, it may be the sheer profusion of nationalist causes toward the end of the century that has devalued the religion of na-tionalism and created unbelievers. As the century closes it may also be the weight of lost patriots and patriots lost that leads to disbelief among youth in many parts of the world that they de-serve such a fate. Cynicism or enlight-enment? A total collapse of societal val-ues and national pride or an unin-tended gift of this century to the next?

Charles C. Stewart

Terrorism

Shot down on the streets of Algiers in the 1950s, this victim of terrorist bullets exposes the impotence of the police who stand about the body after arriving too late to protect the victim or catch the gunman. In the attitude of the authorities as well as the fate of the victim we can read our own bewilderment at being held hostage to causes foreign and causes that seem to crowd headlines increasingly as the century comes to a close. Are such shootings criminal attacks against the innocent or the legitimate tactics of the desperate weak to undermine the bullying strong? Is this war on its most elemental level? In Algeria and Israel, Kenya and South Africa, terrorists played important roles in independence movements, and individuals condemned as terrorists one day led nations the next. Terrorism and idealism are disturbingly close. At the end of the twentieth century, terrorists in the postcolonial state act in the name of religious purity, giving holy justification to very unholy acts.

Terrorism is a quintessential product of this century insofar as its main object is psychological rather than physical damage. Politically, terrorism assaults the mind, eroding security and dissolving confidence. By exposing the vulnerabilities of everyday life on city streets, terrorism can unsettle an entire population. Its power comes from the haunting fact that it is easier to destroy than to create; a life is a miracle, while a bullet is mundane.

Terrorism has been most prevalent in the developing world, but it is state governments in the developed world that most fear attack. The complexity of life in the city, its patterns and infrastructure, its symbols and international links, makes it a perfect target; moreover, societies which are jealous of political freedom and personal privacy give terrorists the room to operate. Moreover, the great killing power of sophisticated modern military weaponry is particularly ill suited to dealing with terrorists, whose success is frequently the product of the most basic weapons: pistols, plastic, and pipe bombs.

By the end of the century the terrorist's arsenal includes far more advanced weapons; a truck bomb erases a building, and the lives within it. Even weapons of mass destruction have entered the terrorist arsenal. Zealots poison the Tokyo subway with Seren gas, while the ultimate threat, nuclear terrorism, seems disturbingly close. The single mid-century victim pictured here could be multiplied by the mathematics of fanaticism, so that security in the twenty-first century may become a fragile thing.

John A. Lynn

René Vital/Archive Photos

137

United Nations

This picture of United Nations peace-keepers happens to come from Cyprus, but its very anonymity, possibly taken from any of several dozen like missions during the second half of the century, testifies to a widespread impression that this has been a century of violence and international disruptions. Certainly the horrors of two world wars and other great conflicts, the perils and tensions of the nuclear arms race in the cold war, and the persistence of widespread civil war, fratricidal ethnic conflict, and even genocide since the end of the cold war make such a verdict understandable. Yet as an appraisal of the whole century from a historical perspective, and in comparison to others, this image of the century is very misleading.

In fact, during the latter half of this century (since 1953) there has been a longer, more durable general peace (i.e., no wars directly between major global powers, much less any general systemic war) on this planet than at any time since the Roman Empire. In this century an international organization, the United Nations, representing all the countries of the world, has not only endured for five decades but has also grown in effectiveness, reach, and breadth of functions. In this century, alliances such as NATO since 1949 have not only proved far more durable and coherent than ever before but they have steadily expanded their functions beyond purely military and security purposes to economic, political, and even cultural cooperation and coordination of policy, including the promotion of civil rights.

In the latter part of this century, the big fish are no longer eating the little fish, but the little fish are swimming beside the big fish, sometimes going off in independent channels by themselves. In this century, all the great colonial empires have been broken up, mostly peacefully and voluntarily. And more new states have been formed by the resulting independence movements, mainly peacefully, than in any other. In this century, far more political and economic integration and cooperation has been achieved between independent states, above all the most developed ones, than ever before.

In this century, far more countries and peoples than ever before have accepted the necessity and value of legitimating state power and governmental authority through democratic elections. Coups, military dictatorships, and other forms of authoritarianism still occur, but they are no longer the norm, and even they must claim to be subscribing to democratic mores.

In this century, despite obvious failures, there has been more widespread and effective international intervention to stop aggression and to end international or civil wars than ever before. It is for this reason that this image looks so very familiar to us. At the same time, the international community now has more effective nonmilitary sanctions than ever before (economic pressures, denial of membership in international or regional organizations, nonrecognition, worldwide publicity, pressure from nongovernmental organizations, etc.) to use for deterrence, persuasion, and conciliation.

In this century, as never before, great powers have not only bowed to an international, moral pressure and accepted failure and defeat in armed conflicts with smaller powers rather than continue unpopular wars; they have also given up the attempt to retain their rank as great powers without a fight, and have been allowed to do so without inviting their own destruction.

Does all this mean that international problems have been solved, the old dangers and disorder are past? Certainly not. Old problems persist, and grave new ones are arising from population pressures, pressures on resources and the environment, and the breakup of fragile states, to name but the obvious. Yet to ignore the remarkable advances we have witnessed in international politics in this century is akin to suggesting that the presence of new deadly disease in our societies is an indication that medical science has made no advances. The twentieth century has been one of terrible violence, but it also has been one of undeniable, breathtaking international advance by comparison to any earlier era. It has been, to paraphrase Dickens, the worst of times and the best of times.

Paul W. Schroeder

139

140

Water

Water, Water, Everywhere . . . Stranded freighters in what was once the Aral Sea, a vast fresh-water lake in what was once the Soviet Union, bear stark witness to environmental catastrophe. Now bordered by the independent republics of Kazakhstan and Uzbekistan, the lake has been split in two and reduced to half its former size, the victim of massive irrigation schemes in the 1960s designed to grow cotton. There *are* limits to how far we can exploit nature.

I grew up in Toronto. The city sits on Lake Ontario and its hinterland, barely one hundred miles north, starting in the district of Muskoka, consists largely of the Canadian Shield, a vast formation of bedrock scoured by glaciers, and holding, we were told, half of the world's supply of fresh water. Growing up we canoed and camped in that country. We came to understand art through our enthusiasm for the Group of Seven, painters who celebrated the lakes and woods of the northland. It was unthinkable in the 1950s that water should ever be a problem. Yet, looking back I realize that we rarely swam in Lake Ontario. Not only was it cold, everybody knew it was "polluted." In those days we understood pollution in terms of bacteria levels. Today we also know that the industrial waste dumped into the lake is carcinogenic. What is more, acid rain now afflicts Muskoka's fish and forests.

It is hard for us not to treat water as a free good, as plentiful as it is necessary. One hundred years ago, our ancestors used water to generate steam and steam, in turn, powered the first factories of the modern world. Steamship lines reached from continent to continent and built Europe's extraordinary maritime empires. Steam locomotives opened the interiors of continents to soldiers, teachers, and traders from the metropoles. Rail lines evacuated the mineral and agricultural wealth of the colonies. Waterways have always been among the great triumphs of engineering: the Suez and Panama canals, and later in the century, the Grand Coulee and Aswan dams. While steam no longer runs factories, we still need water to make electrical power, whatever the energy source. In India, the Middle East, and the American West, we divert scarce water to irrigate gardens in the desert. And we continue to use water and waterways to dispose of waste. Perhaps one of this century's most enduring legacies will be the price that has come to be levied on this "free good."

"Water, water, every where, / Nor any drop to drink."

Donald E. Crummey

Amazonia

" . . . the tranquil waterway leading to the uttermost ends of the earth flowed somber under an overcast sky— seemed to lead into the heart of an immense darkness."

Joseph Conrad's 1902 tale of extreme horror, tyrannical power, and self-recognition, *The Heart of Darkness,* was set on the Congo River in the "savage" central African jungles, yet the title itself derived from a famous 1890s moralistic reform tract about the horrors of London's industrial slums. The Congo, New Guinea, Amazonia, where paradisical beauty and savage horrors combine in the "last frontiers of humanity," are intricately linked to the modern, "western" penetration of the jungle. These are the sites that conjure up images of untapped treasure, terrifying adventure, and wild Stone Age tribes. Amazonia has been imagined in this way since the sixteenth century, but twentieth-century civilization has cut many swaths into this idea. Still, it remains a vast frontier, where the realities of beauty, bounty, and horror are propelled to fantastic heights by unbridled modern imagination.

Serra Pelada, one contemporary image of hell, is the largest open-pit gold mine in the world. Located in the state of Pará, Brazil, it is organized as a "democratic co-operative" of *garimpeiros* (gold diggers), who discovered the deposit in 1979. In reality it is controlled by a few of the richest among them, with connections to large mining corporations and urban capitalists, and it is run like a huge slave camp, where tens of thousands of desperate men, from the shantytowns of Sao Paulo and the dirt-poor backlands of the arid northeast, see their dreams of getting rich fast converted into twelve-hour days of backbreaking work, disease, physical punishment, and death. But the gold diggers of Amazonia, in Brazil as much as in Peru, Colombia, and Bolivia, easily turn from victims into aggressors. Panning gold in remote river valleys, they invade territories set aside for Amazon Indian tribes like the Yanomami, bring disease, force the men of the tribes to work for them, rape the women, and destroy entire villages.

The first wave in the modern conquest of Amazonia began about a century ago, with the collection of wild rubber, raw material for automobile tires. Tens of thousands of native Amazonians were dispatched to tap trees, and terror and executions became tools for achieving labor discipline. Throughout the twentieth century the advancing Amazonian frontier, disseminating "modern civilization" first along the river valleys, then along a few railroad paths leading to nowhere, then through the transamazon highway and thousands of airplane landing strips cut into the jungle, has produced a steady series of apocalyptic horrors.

Yet beauty and healing take on fantastic dimensions in Amazonia as well.

Collart/Odinetz/Gamma Liaison

143

Tif Hunter/Tony Stone

The plumage of the arara (parrot) and the toucan is spectacular. The endless variety of flora and fauna offers a storehouse of wonderfully adaptive behaviors and genetic codes. The powerful creation myths of the Amazon peoples beautifully evoke the connectedness between humankind and other living species. The spiritual and physical healing powers of their shamans combine ritual with the unique pharmacopoeia of the region's plants and animals. And now Amazonia is expected to become a global healer, as oxygen pump for a polluted world and as provider of 20 percent of a thirsty humanity's fresh water supply.

Home of vibrant yet endangered native cultures, vital territory for the nation-states of Brazil and its Andean neighbors, Amazonia is more and more cast as the patrimony of humanity. The heart of darkness also calls forth images of light: of beauty and hope, of healing and redemption. The question will be whether this realm, encompassing nearly 5 percent of the world's land mass, can contain all the contradictory hopes and aspirations that are projected upon it. If all of these are to be realized in part, will Amazonia not have to cease being the domain of the fantastic and of horror?

Nils P. Jacobsen

Medical Machines

The nineteenth-century love and fear of machinery has become much more intimate in the late twentieth century as medical machines have moved into the hospital and from the hospital into the home and become, literally, attached to the sickbed. The picture of the dangerously ill person in bed aided by machinery represents at once the best hopes and the worst fears of many. The metallic gleam of medical equipment, the hum, clicks, and alarms of computer-aided IV feedings, the tubes connecting the machine to the human body promise health and recovery. Yet, at the same time, they invoke sleeplessness, anxiety, and a renewed sense of the need for the human touch.

The new machinery developed in the late nineteenth and twentieth centuries—the x-ray machine, the incubator, the respirator, and many more—helped to move patient care, childbirth, and death from the home to the hospital. As objects, machines have been adopted by medical practitioners as critical to their abilities to save lives, proofs of their attachment to science, and symbols of their modernity. Some machines have been embraced that have proven to have dangerous effects, such as the x-ray machine, which induced new cancers and disfigured practitioners. With the fetal monitor, an expensive machine has replaced an equally effective and older technology, the stethoscope, and has resulted in unnecessary operations. Nonetheless, at least in the Western context, it has become difficult for many physicians to detach themselves from their reliance on the machine.

The benefits of medical technology are by no means distributed equally. Those without health insurance in the United States and citizens in poor, underdeveloped countries may have no access to high-tech care. Poor and minority Americans worry that technological assistance that could preserve their lives will be denied them (or, if expensive technological care is offered, they fear they may be subjected to scientific experiments, as they indeed were in the recent past). The fear of being attached to a machine for too long is largely a luxury of the privileged and the well-insured.

Patients have contradictory attitudes toward medical technology. Patients want machines to save them, yet many, as the recent popularization of living wills indicates, are deeply afraid of being attached to machinery and forced to "live" in a debilitated state. The difficult question that faces the sick and injured, families, and health care providers, is determining when life-support machinery might help the patient to return to a full life and when it will only produce pain and prolong the process of dying.

The twentieth century opened in the West with excitement about the possibilities of medicine and the beginnings of the mass movement into the hospital. It ends with unexpected concerns, as medical machines contribute to uncomfortable hospital environments and inspire patients to remove themselves from the hospital to seek the comforts of home, for both birthing and dying.

Leslie J. Reagan

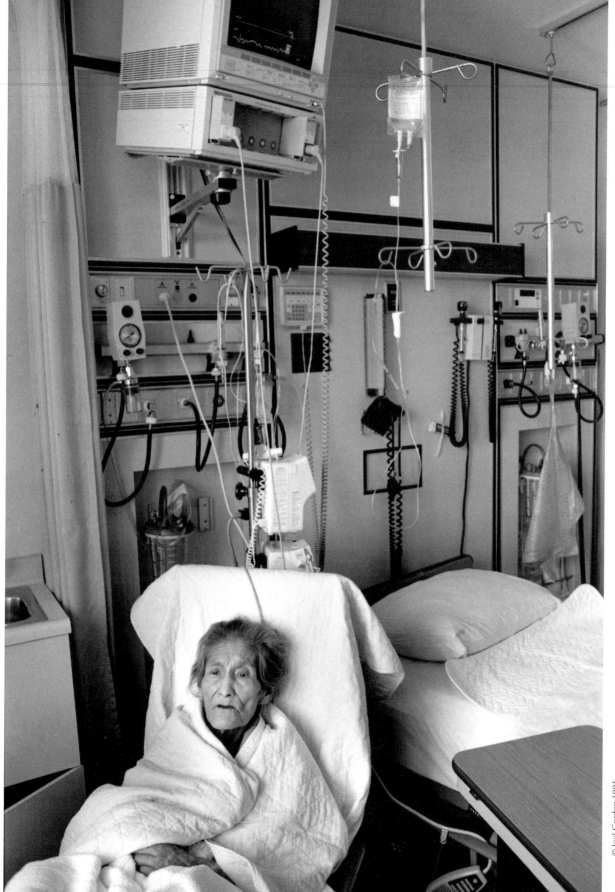

David Harry Stewart/Tony Stone

Aging

A specter has been haunting the twentieth century: the specter of age conflict. The twentieth has a greater proportion of older citizens than any century previous and political debates over scarce resources have increasingly adopted the terms of generational warfare: will the budgetary deficits racked up by the older generation doom the prosperity of the young? Will the welfare of the young be devastated by the need to support ever larger numbers of nonproductive elderly? Will families assist aging parents as effectively as they nurture young children?

Predictions that young and old would square off against one another have emerged over the course of the century as it has become clear that populations are simply living longer. It is a commonplace to see friends and acquaintances live past the biblical lifetime of seventy years. In the United States, for example, 3 million people were over the age of 65 in 1900, 4 percent of the population. By 1980, this figure had risen to 25 million, 11 percent of the population. In 1900, two-thirds of men over 65 were gainfully employed, but by 1980, only one-fifth

were. As early as 1920, policymakers recognized that American society was aging and began to devise programs and fields of study to explore the implications of this phenomenon.

Generational consciousness was first spurred on by perceived demographic changes, and it has been reinforced through the century by the very programs developed to ease generational conflict. The Social Security Act (1934) instilled a sense of old age as a stage in the life cycle that was especially vulnerable and deserving of social support. Retirement or old age pensions, bestowed early in the century as rewards for especially deserving employees, came to be viewed as entitlements earned not by individual merit but by virtue of age alone. Powerful lobby groups such as the American Association of Retired Persons have kept these entitlements in place. Although the prosperous industrialized West can afford them, the programs to transfer wealth from the producers to former producers has fashioned a sense of the separateness of the elderly. The creation of new fields of study—the medical specialty of geriatrics, the social science

field of gerontology—have made these divisions even more marked.

The elderly were in large part created by advances in modern medicine and made distinct as a category by social institutions, but the twentieth century has also revealed how various are the experiences of being old. Men and women age rather differently, so do the active and the infirm, and those in industrial and developing societies. Moreover, many of the assumptions of generational conflict have been based on impressions rather than fact. The happy yesteryears when several generations lived in one household turn out never to have existed, and only a minority of the elderly today are truly cut off from the younger generation. "Intimacy at a distance" is more common than true generational cleavage. Baby boomers will undoubtedly sponsor old age as their next project.

Nonetheless, it is ironic that the century that was inaugurated as the "century of the child" concludes with economic and political power firmly in the hands of the elderly.

Diane P. Koenkers

Anticipation

Starry, fragrant nights, quiet talk on the front porch; passing the time of day across the back fence. Holiday waits for oversized packages, grandparents' visits, and special smells, starchy, scrubbed stiffness. Berry picking, apple paring, two warm cherry pies; children taking turns on the ice cream churn on a hot summer's day. Canvas lounge chairs on a sunny deck, five days' sail toward Southampton. Fear of the dreaded telegram from headquarters and its uniformed bearer. Joy of the trainside reunion of soldier and lover, child and father. The first coquettish snowflake drifting toward ground, herald of winter glitter. Courting and poems, strolls to nowhere and numbing silence, restlessness, daydreaming, impatience, heartsickness. Drudgery of factory floor, tighten and pull; household wash, bake and scrub; school memorization, uniforms and orders; office routine, smiles on demand; paychecks. Wonder and awe of love, of bodies, of creation, of children, of growing, of dying. Young ballerina's first stage performance, a peek at the audience through a discretely parted curtain.

Fast forward. Instant cure. Real-time visits. Web-site teachers. Voice-mail parents. Fast lane. Instant photos. Accelerated learning. Instant entertainment. Bullet trains. TGV. Fast women. Fast food. Internet. Fast relief. Concorde. Twelve-step cures. Speed. Fast record. E-mail. Instant banking. Dating service. Mail-order brides. Fast tan. Quick Copy. Instant coffee. Fast cars. Quickie. Electronic texts, paperless society. Quick germination. Books on tape. Microwaves. Satellite weather. Instant justice. While you wait. 24-hour service.

Our sense of anticipation has changed in the twentieth century. The subject of anticipation now is the speed of change rather than the change of speed. We are more efficient, we can accomplish more in a day than could our parents and they more than their parents. There is little time or space between the unknown and the known in quotidian life, and despite the savings in time we accumulate, we mourn the loss of time to anticipate and to savor the future.

In Saint-Exupéry's *The Little Prince,* his unearthly subject is introduced to a merchant who sells pills which would quench thirst for one full week. When he asks why, the little prince is told that experts compute a savings of fifty-three minutes in every week the pills are taken.

"And what do I do with those fifty-three minutes?"

"Anything you like . . ."

"As for me," said the little prince to himself, "if I had fifty-three minutes to spend as I liked, I should walk at my leisure towards a spring of fresh water."

Charles C. Stewart

Desmond Burdon/Tony Stone

The Haircut

In the turbulent sea of twentieth-century change the ordinary haircut endures as an island of tranquillity. As in 1900, today's barber carefully cuts and clips men's hair with traditional tools (and electrified clippers) for about a quarter of an hour. Conversation and humor embellish craft and custom, and an easy sociability reigns in the well-run shop. Moreover, the haircut is the result of the same quick movements carried out in roughly the same amount of time throughout the world.

Of course, it is easy to spot certain changes in the hair-cutting trade. Many barbers are now women, especially in Europe. And prices vary enormously between Paris, France, and Paris, Illinois, and they have risen rather steeply since this gentleman paid for his haircut in coin at Vincent's barbershop on New York's West Eighth Street in 1943. Yet on closer examination the real price really has not changed much over time and space. This stability in the face of so much change well reflects the ambiguous nature of the epochal improvement in living conditions that we have seen in industrialized countries since the late 1940s.

The true impact of price changes is difficult to measure because the twentieth century has been an era of monstrous inflation for most countries. Since 1913, French prices, for example, have risen more than one hundred times as fast as those in the United States. What then can serve as a meaningful measure of value when the value of money itself is in chaos? For the French economist Jean Fourastié the answer lay in reliable historical data on the daily wages of unskilled adult male workers in France. Using this wage as a measuring rod, Fourastié could state the price of all goods and services in terms of a basic reality—the work of adult males from the poorest classes.

Now we can price the haircut. Throughout the twentieth century the ordinary (predominately scissors) haircut for a French male has cost a little more or a little less than the wage paid to an unskilled adult male for one hour of work. What accounts for this price stability? The standard haircut is a classic example of a labor-intensive service that has experienced little technical progress. The barber still takes fifteen minutes to serve the client; he (or she) cannot reduce the real price, either in France or around the world. A stark contrast is offered by the production costs associated with the glass mirror, so beloved by King Louis XIV as a symbol of awesome extravagance. This product (like the one in Vincent's) has benefited spectacularly from technical progress and increased labor productivity. In France in 1985, a square meter of glass mirror cost 7.5 hours of wages of unskilled labor, as opposed to about 200 hours in 1960 (and 40,000 hours in 1702).

Haircut and mirror: two faces of the twentieth-century world. One a changeless service at a traditional price; the other, one of innumerable luxury items transformed by the alchemy of technology and increased productivity into bagatelles of mass consumption. Fourastié's point is well made.

Yet the mirror also reflects back to the haircut and on out to other satisfying "labor-intensive services"—a leisurely dinner, a talk with a friend, a story with a child, an hour with a loved one. Such services—precious experiences really—are seldom mechanized or speeded up without being devalued. Thus the actual and potential contribution of technical progress to human well-being is clearly limited. The two-minute shearing of an army recruit is not a haircut.

John P. McKay

Earthrise

There is a wonderful children's book in which a series of photographs pinpoint a red balloon in a little boy's hand in increasingly larger frames. Page by page, the balloon gets smaller and smaller and soon disappears altogether as the perspective grows more and more distant. Balloon, backyard, city block, neighborhood, metropolis, region, coastline—finally all we can make out are the cloud-fringed outlines of continents on the surface of the earth swimming in space. To flip the pages of the book is to chart a peculiarly twentieth-century trajectory. The view of the earth from outer space was possible only with the development of rocketry. Indeed, the first images of "earthrise" date only from the *Voyager* expeditions in the late 1960s.

The image of a distant earth has a certain familiarity about it. Each technological development, from coast-hugging traders to oceangoing steamers, from rickety airplanes to solid-fuel rockets, has extended the horizon of the known world. Over the course of the last hundred years, maps that had once depicted shorelines and harbors came to illustrate continents and airports and finally, with space travel, planets and galaxies. In this progression, "Earthrise" appears as a triumphal expression of the potentialities and improvement of humankind.

"Earthrise" is also unremarkable because we are accustomed to operate in many social contexts and our identity

National Aeronautics and Space Administration

as earth-beings is as recognizable to us as our allegiance to neighborhood or nation. To flip the pages of the picture book is an exercise in experiencing the multiple selves that we inhabit. We feel loyalties to home and backyard, and also to neighborhood and country. At the same time, we feel the pull of a more encompassing allegiance to the earth and its survival. Over the course of the twentieth century, the carnage of two world wars, the threat of nuclear holocaust, and the ecological devastation of relentless industrial development have strengthened the legitimacy of international organizations from the United Nations to Greenpeace and made global issues such as deforestation, arms control, and ozone depletion more compelling. "Earthrise" does not recognize national borders. It thereby generates a sense of humility in the face of grand political projects and it tugs at common bonds and shared needs. It is a cherished end point to present-day efforts to overcome the fatalities of nationalism and to manage natural resources more carefully.

And yet "Earthrise" is also a profoundly disturbing and unfamiliar picture. It is as if the visualized planet has effaced our social and political world. "Earthrise" could be a picture of the earth either still before the first appearance of hominids or already after an all-out nuclear war. The image is impervious to human work, to traditions, to memories. To look at "Earthrise" is to be unable to find a place for our great fears and collective aspirations. In this sense, it is a blinding, destructive source of light. Indeed, the philosopher Martin Heidegger remarked that the images of the *Voyager* probe were more frightful to him than even the dystopian possibility of atomic warfare; "Earthrise" did not include or retrieve a sense of human being.

But there *are* people in "Earthrise." They cannot be placed in the image itself but they are implicit in it. The photograph is itself a product of an extremely complex technological process of probes, radio signals, and computers. Although the earth appears to be free of all technical mediation—not a single city or polluted valley can be identified—"Earthrise" insists on a technical presence. Our photograph and our earth convey two messages. They depict the inconsequentiality of human works and, at the same time, indicate an end point in the manifestation of human power. Given the circumstances of its production, "Earthrise" generates as much hubris as humility. We might ask whether the *Voyager* project has not confirmed the ability of human beings to set the terms of representation and, if that is the case, doesn't it point to a future in which men and women are always in the picture, neither lost nor saved?

Peter Fritzsche

Further Readings
and Contributors

Further Readings

Private Histories: Michelle Perrot, ed., *A History of Private Life* (Cambridge, 1994).

Birth of a New Age: Lester Brown, *Full House: Reassessing the Earth's Population Carrying Capacity* (New York, 1994).

Childhood: Harvey Graff, *Conflicting Paths: Growing Up in America* (Cambridge, 1995).

Servants: John Burnett, *A History of the Cost of Living* (Harmondsworth, 1969).

Ethnicity: Walker Connor, *Ethnonationalism: The Quest for Understanding* (Princeton, 1994).

Anachronism: Stuart Ewen, *All Consuming Images: The Politics of Style in Contemporary Culture* (New York, 1988).

First Car: Ilya Ehrenburg, *The Life of the Automobile* (New York, 1990).

Bridges: David J. Brown, *Bridges* (New York, 1993).

History of the Future: Mark Hillegas, *The Future as Nightmare: H. G. Wells and the Anti-Utopians* (Carbondale, Ill., 1974).

The Merry-Go-Round: Paul Fussell, *The Great War and Modern Memory* (New York, 1975).

Disillusion: John Keegan, *Face of Battle* (New York, 1976).

Lenin's Light Bulb: John Scott, *Behind the Urals: An American Worker in Russia*, enlarged ed. (Bloomington, Ind., 1989).

Imperialism: Daniel R. Headrick, *Tools of Empire: Technology and European Imperialism in the Nineteenth Century* (New York, 1981).

Gandhi: Dennis Dalton, *Gandhi: Nonviolent Power and Action* (New York, 1993).

Jersey Shore: Kathy Peiss, *Cheap Amusements: Working Women and Leisure in Turn-of-the-Century New York* (Philadelphia, 1986).

Music: Paul Griffiths, *A Concise History of Avant-garde Music* (Oxford, 1978).

Intolerance: Robert A. Goldberg, *Grassroots Resistance: Social Movements in Twentieth-Century America* (Belmont, Calif., 1991).

A Nisei in the Andes: Luis Jochamowitz, *Ciudadano Fujimori* (Lima, 1993).

Typist: Sharon Strom, *Beyond the Typewriter: Gender, Class, and the Origins of Modern American Office Work, 1900–1930* (Urbana, Ill., 1992).

Freud: Sigmund Freud, *Civilization and Its Discontents* (London, 1930).

The Crowd: Elias Canetti, *Crowds and Power* (New York, 1962).

The Spanish Civil War: Ronald Fraser, *Blood of Spain: An Oral History of the Spanish Civil War* (New York, 1979).

No Work: Studs Terkel, *Hard Times: An Oral History of the Great Depression* (New York, 1970).

Individualism: Lawrence W. Levine, *The Unpredictable Past* (New York, 1993).

Fallingwater: *Architectural Digest* (1991).

World's Fair: David Gelernter, *1939: The Lost World of the Fair* (New York, 1995).

Olympics: Sebastian Coe, *The Olympians: A Quest for Gold. Triumphs, Heroes, and Legends* (London, 1994).

Chaplin: Charles Chaplin, *My Autobiography* (New York, 1964).

Women's War: Karen Anderson, *Wartime Women* (Westport, Conn., 1981).

Mass Death: John Hersey, *Hiroshima* (New York, 1989).

The Holocaust: Peter Weiss, *The Investigation* (London, 1966).

Transistor: Michael Riordan and Lillian Hoddeson, *Crystal Fire: The Birth of the Information Age* (New York, 1997).

Migrants: Stephen Castles and Mark J. Miller, *The Age of Migration: International Population Movements in the Modern World* (New York, 1993).

Evita Perón: Tomas Eloy Martinez, *Santa Evita* (New York, 1996).

Barbie: Miriam Formanek-Brunell, *Made to Play House: Dolls and the Commercialization of American Girlhood, 1830–1930* (New Haven, 1993).

Movie Audience: Robert Sklar, *Movie-Made America: A Cultural History of American Movies* (New York, 1994).

Icons of Empire: Brian Lapping, *End of Empire* (New York, 1985).

Kenyatta: Jomo Kenyatta, *Facing Mount Kenya* (London, 1953).

Cold War: N. S. Khrushchev, *Khrushchev Remembers* (Boston, 1970).

Atomic Age: Paul S. Boyer, *By the Bomb's Early Light: American Thought and Culture at the Dawn of the Atomic Age* (New York, 1985).

Decolonization: Daniel A. Offiong, *Imperialism and Dependency: Obstacles to African Development* (Washington, D.C., 1982).

Black over White?: Frantz Fanon, *The Wretched of the Earth* (New York, 1963).

Islam: John O. Voll, *Islam: Continuity and Change in the Modern World* (Syracuse, N.Y., 1994).

The Pope in Africa: John Esposito, *The Islamic Threat: Myth or Reality?* (New York, 1992).

The Green Revolution: Lester Brown, *The Seeds of Change: The Green Revolution and Development in the 1970s* (New York, 1970).

Abundance: John Kenneth Galbraith, *The Affluent Society* (Boston, 1958).

Suburbs: Elaine Tyler May, *Homeward Bound: American Families in the Cold War Era* (New York, 1988).

The Pill: Linda Gordon, *Woman's Body, Woman's Right: Birth Control in America* (New York, 1990).

TV: Lynn Spigel, *Make Room for TV: Television and the Family Ideal in Postwar America* (Chicago, 1992).

Marketplace: Paul Bairoch, *Economics and World History: Myths and Paradoxes* (Chicago, 1993).

Airplane Eye: Leo Marx, *The Machine in the Garden: Technology and the Pastoral Ideal in America* (New York, 1964).

Machines and Work: Richard Edwards, *Contested Terrain: The Transformation of the Workplace in the Twentieth Century* (New York, 1979).

Plastics: Rachel Carson, *Silent Spring* (Boston, 1962).

Refugees: United Nations High Commissioner for Refugees, *The State of the World's Refugees 1995: In Search of Solutions* (New York, 1995).

Counterculture: Theodore Roszak, *The Making of a Counter Culture* (New York, 1969).

Jukebox: Simon Reynolds and Joy Press, *The Sex Revolts: Gender, Rebellion and Rock 'n' Roll* (Cambridge, 1996).

Kung Fu Films: Lau Shing-hon, *A Study of the Hong Kong Martial Arts Film* (Hong Kong, 1980).

Tokyo: Edward Seidenstücker, *Tokyo Rising: The City since the Great Earthquake* (New York, 1990).

Creating Race: James Moy, *Marginal Sights: Staging the Chinese in America* (Iowa City, 1993).

End of Communism: David Remnick, *Lenin's Tomb: Last Days of the Soviet Empire* (New York, 1993).

Human Rights: Michael Davis, *Human Rights and Chinese Values* (Oxford, 1995).

Behind the Veil: Sherifa Zuhur, *Revealing Reveiling: Islamist Gender Ideology in Contemporary Egypt* (Albany, N.Y., 1992).

Redrawing the Globe: Harold Nicolson, *Peacemaking 1919* (London, 1933).

Lost Patriots: Jean Larteguy, *The Centurions* (New York, 1962).

Terrorism: Alistair Horne, *A Savage War of Peace: Algeria 1954–1962* (London, 1977).

United Nations: John Mueller, *Retreat from Doomsday: The Obsolescence of Major War* (New York, 1989).

Water: Norman Maclean, *A River Runs through It* (Chicago, 1983).

Amazonia: Alejo Carpentier, *The Lost Steps* (New York, 1989).

Medical Machines: Joel D. Howell, *Technology in the Hospital: Transforming Patient Care in the Early Twentieth Century* (Baltimore, 1995).

Aging: W. Andrew Aschenbaum, *Shades of Gray: Old Age, American Values and Federal Policies since 1920* (Boston, 1983).

Anticipation: Antoine de Saint-Exupéry, *The Little Prince* (New York, 1943).

The Haircut: Jean Fourastié, *The Causes of Wealth* (Glencoe, Ill., 1960).

Earthrise: Walter A. McDougall, *. . . the Heavens and the Earth: A Political History of the Space Age* (New York, 1985).

Contributors

Walter L. Arnstein, Professor of History since 1968 and Jubilee Professor of the Liberal Arts and Sciences since 1989, is the author or editor of six books and of more than thirty scholarly articles including *Britain Yesterday and Today: 1830 to the Present* (Lexington), of which a seventh edition was published in 1996.

James R. Barrett's books include *Work and Community in the Jungle: Chicago's Packinghouse Workers* (Urbana, 1987) and, with Steve Nelson and Rob Ruck, *Steve Nelson, American Radical* (Pittsburgh, 1981). He has recently completed *William Z. Foster and the Tragedy of American Communism* and is writing a book of essays on the identities, consciousness, and private lives of working people in the twentieth-century United States.

Donald E. Crummey holds degrees from the University of Toronto and London University. He lived for six years in Ethiopia, before joining the faculty of the University of Illinois in 1973. He is married, has three children, and is an Episcopalian. He has maintained Ethiopia as his principal research focus. A book on historic land tenure in that country is in press; a project on environmental history is ongoing; and a return to the study of Ethiopia's religious institutions seems likely.

Kenneth M. Cuno received his Ph.D. in history from UCLA in 1985 and taught for several years at the American University in Cairo before joining the faculty at the University of Illinois at Urbana-Champaign in 1990. He teaches a variety of topics in the history of the Middle East. His primary research interest is the social history of modern Egypt and his publications include *The Pasha's Peasants: Land, Society, and Economy in Lower Egypt, 1740–1858* (Cambridge, 1992).

Kevin M. Doak teaches history and East Asian civilizations. He is the author of *Dreams of Difference: The Japan Romantic School and the Crisis of Modernity* (Berkeley, 1994) and numerous articles on nationalism, ethnicity, and social identity in modern Japan.

A 1986 Ph.D. from the University of California, Berkeley, Peter Fritzsche teaches modern European history and is the author *Rehearsals for Fascism: Populism and Political Mobilization in Weimar Germany* (New York, 1990); *A Nation of Fliers: German Aviation and the Popular Imagination* (Cambridge, 1992); *Reading Berlin 1900* (Cambridge, 1996); and *Germans into Nazis* (Cambridge, forthcoming). He is currently at work on a history of nostalgia.

Poshek Fu is a diasporic, bicultural person. He was born in Hong Kong, educated in North America, and has worked in Canada, China, Hong Kong, and the United States. A film critic, martial arts enthusiast, political commentator, and college teacher, he has devoted his writings to recovering suppressed voices in history. His most recent book is *Passivity, Resistance, and Collaboration: Intellectual Choices in Occupied Shanghai, 1937–1945* (Stanford, 1993).

Nils P. Jacobsen has published a monograph, two edited anthologies, and a number of articles on the history of Peru between the late colonial period and the mid–twentieth century. He is currently working on a book about a Peruvian civil war in the 1890s, in which he explores the meaning of revolution in Latin America.

Blair B. Kling specializes in modern Indian history. He teaches courses on South Asia and has written on peasant movements, business and entrepreneurship, Mahatma Gandhi, and Rabindranath Tagore.

Diane P. Koenker has written widely on revolutionary Russia and on Russian working-class history, and most recently edited *Revelations from the Russian Archives* (Washington, D.C., 1997). She teaches Russian and Soviet history, and the history of the European working class.

Mark H. Leff, whose writings include *The Limits of Symbolic Reform* (Cambridge, 1984) and "Revisioning U.S. Political History" (*American Historical Review*, June 1995), has long peddled himself as a "historian of U.S. public policy and society in the twentieth century." He thus faces a fin-de-siècle crisis at the prospect of reconfiguring his "field" once his teaching responsibilities extend into the twenty-first century.

John A. Lynn, Professor of History at the University of Illinois at Urbana-Champaign, is a specialist in military history who devotes most of his attention to French military institutions. His works include *Giant of the Grand Siècle: The French Army, 1610–1715* (New York, 1997) and *The Bayonets of the Republic: Motivation and Tactics in the Army of Revolutionary France, 1791–94 (Chicago, 1996)*. He also held the Oppenheimer Chair of Warfighting Strategy at the Marine Corps University, Quantico, Va., 1994–95.

John P. McKay began his academic journey with the study of European economic and social history. He has written four books in this field, including *Pioneers for Profit: Foreign Entrepreneurship and Russian Industrialization, 1885-1913* (Chicago, 1970), which won the American Historical Association's Herbert Baxter Adams prize in European history. He is also a co-author of *A History of World Societies*, whose fourth edition was published by Houghton Mifflin in 1996.

Kathryn J. Oberdeck teaches American cultural history at the University of Illinois at Urbana-Champaign. Her scholarship includes several articles and a book in progress focusing on popular culture, popular religion, and competing meanings of culture in American life.

Leslie J. Reagan is the author of the prize-winning *When Abortion Was a Crime: Women, Medicine, and Law in the United States, 1867–1973* (Berkeley, 1997). Her current research is on the history of breast cancer, bodily integrity, and American culture. She teaches at the University of Illinois at Urbana-Champaign in the Department of History and the College of Medicine.

Paul W. Schroeder has been Professor of History at the University of Illinois at Urbana-Champaign since 1963, specializing in the history of European and world international relations, German and Central European history, and the theory of history and international relations theory. He has published four books and more than fifty articles, the latest book being *The Transformation of European Politics, 1763–1848* (Oxford, 1994).

Charles C. Stewart has taught in northern Nigeria and Ghana and at the University of Illinois at Urbana-Champaign, and writes about West African societies and Islam in Africa. His publications include *Islam and Social Order in Mauritania* (Oxford, 1973) and *Popular Islam South of the Sahara* (ed.) (Manchester, 1985).